The Place of Book Illumination in Byzantine Art

The Place of
Book Illumination
in Byzantine Art

Kurt Weitzmann
William C. Loerke
Ernst Kitzinger
Hugo Buchthal

The Art Museum, Princeton University
Distributed by Princeton University Press

Designed by Quentin Fiore
Type set by William Clowes & Sons Ltd.
Printed by the Meriden Gravure Company

Library of Congress Catalogue Card Number 74-84574
International Standard Book Number 0-691-03910-0

Distributed by Princeton University Press,
Princeton, New Jersey 08540

Contents

Preface

In April 1973 a notable exhibition of illuminated Greek manuscripts from American collections opened at The Art Museum of Princeton University. The exhibition was designed to honor Professor Kurt Weitzmann on the occasion of his retirement from the Department of Art and Archaeology. The catalogue of the exhibition, numbering sixty-seven manuscripts and single leaves, was prepared by a group of Professor Weitzmann's present and former students and was edited by Gary Vikan.

On the evening of the preview of the exhibition Professor Weitzmann gave a public lecture: "The Study of Byzantine Book Illumination, Past, Present, and Future." This served as an introduction to the symposium held on the following day, 14 April 1973: "The Place of Book Illumination in Byzantine Art." The participants in the symposium, which, like the exhibition itself, was organized as a tribute to Professor Weitzmann, were William C. Loerke, Director of Studies and Professor of Byzantine Art at Dumbarton Oaks; Ernst Kitzinger, A. Kingsley Porter Professor at Harvard University; and Hugo Buchthal, Ailsa Mellon Bruce Professor at New York University.

We are fortunate to be able to bring together for publication in this volume the papers by these four eminent scholars, all of whom address themselves to the theme of the symposium. Yet each author was encouraged to stress his individual approach, and the result is a variety of methodologies. In the introductory chapter Kurt Weitzmann compares the study of Byzantine book illumination to a series of seven widening circles, beginning with that of documentary evidence and moving outward to such peripheral questions as Jewish and Greco-Roman sources. The articles by William Loerke and Ernst Kitzinger—to employ the same imagery—may be said to occupy the fourth circle, which has to do with the relation between book illumination and monumental art; the two essays are in fact complementary, the one considering the "monumental miniature" and the other the "miniature on the wall." The chapter by Hugo Buchthal, on the other hand, clearly falls within the first circle, because it explores a new province in Byzantine book illumination, that is to say the products of scriptoria in Constantinople during the Palaeologan period of the fourteenth century.

The publication of this book has been made possible by a grant from the Publication Fund of the Department of Art and Archaeology. We are grateful to Lynda Hunsucker for her skillful editing of the typescript; to Judith Spear, who copyedited the manuscript; and to Virginia Wageman, Editor for The Art Museum, who has overseen the production of the work.

John Rupert Martin
Chairman, Department of Art and Archaeology
Princeton University

The Place of Book Illumination in Byzantine Art

Kurt Weitzmann

The Study of Byzantine Book Illumination, Past, Present, and Future

To give historical perspective to the study of the vast and complex field of Byzantine book illumination, let us examine how the subject has been and must continue to be developed by discussing the various methodological approaches to the historical process and by probing into the problems of the influence of Byzantine book illumination on other media, its spread into other countries, and its deep roots in pre-Christian cultures. Byzantine miniature painting was, along with mosaics and fresco and icon painting, one of the principal media through which the representational arts of Byzantium found their most eloquent expression. Each of these media has its own purpose and, although they interpenetrate each other, their growth is governed by different sets of rules.

Before entering upon a discussion of the study of Byzantine book illumination, I should like to touch upon the nature and expressiveness of Byzantine miniatures and to choose characteristic examples of six different modes of expression that must be considered the most essential.

1. At an early time the Byzantines developed to great perfection the art of vivid story-telling through pictures.[1] In the sixth-century Vienna Genesis (figs. 1 and 2)[2] the well-known story of Joseph's temptation by Potiphar's wife is

1. K. Weitzmann, "Die Illustration der Septuaginta," *Münchner Jahrbuch der bildenden Kunst* 3-4 (1952-53), pp. 96ff. (reprinted in English, "The Illustration of the Septuagint," *Studies in Classical and Byzantine Manuscript Illumination*, ed. H. L. Kessler [Chicago, 1971], pp. 45ff.). Idem, "The Selection of Texts for Cyclic Illustration in Byzantine Manuscripts," Dumbarton Oaks Colloquium (in press).

2. W. R. v. Hartel and F. Wickhoff, *Die Wiener Genesis* (Vienna, 1895). H. Gerstinger, *Die Wiener Genesis* (Vienna, 1931). P. Buberl, *Die Byzantinischen Handschriften*, vol. 1: *Der Wiener Dioscurides und die Wiener Genesis*, Beschreibendes Verzeichnis der Illuminierten Handschriften in Österreich (Leipzig, 1937), vol. 8, part 4.

Figs. 1–2. Story of Joseph. Vienna, Nationalbibliothek, cod. theol. gr. 31, *picturae* 31–32

dramatically told in a rapid sequence of scenes. Potiphar's wife, posed seductively on a couch, grasps the cloak of Joseph, who flees in alarm, calming down as soon as he passes the threshold. Then Potiphar's wife, in the presence of a vicious-looking companion, makes her false accusations when her husband has hurried home as if with some foreboding; immediately then the accomplice holds out Joseph's cloak to the irate Potiphar. One can "read" this picture story without resorting to the text for explanation, and herein lie the roots of an art that has reached perfection in our own time in the motion picture.

2. In Byzantine hieratic compositions is seen the greatest possible contrast to such vivid action. Ultimately derived from the ancient Orient, such compositions properly express dignity, remoteness, awe, and sanctity in a Christian culture. An evangelist such as John in one of Princeton's Gospel books from Andreaskiti on Mount Athos (fig. 3)[3] shows a certain degree of abstraction in the design of the garments, an intentional restraint of motion, and a strict frontality that are shared by all figures, not only in this and similar manuscripts, but in monumental and icon art as well.

3. As if sensing that the hieratic formula might crystallize into the stereotype, the routine, or the lifeless, Byzantine art revitalized itself in the post-Iconoclastic period by copying good classical models. In a Gospel book at Stauronikita on Mount Athos, Matthew (fig. 4)[4] is depicted as a philosopher, deep in thought in a statue-like pose, and with facial features so faithful to the model that it can be identified as Epicurus.[5] This reintroduction of the classical mode originated in book illumination. It is connected with a revival of classical learning centered at the court of certain emperors of the Macedonian dynasty, and has thus been termed the Macedonian Renaissance.[6] The impact of this movement was so great that, although it became modified, the classical mode never again went entirely out of fashion.

3. K. Weitzmann, *Die byzantinische Buchmalerei des IX. und X. Jahrhunderts* (Berlin, 1935), p. 56 and pl. 63, figs. 374–78. *Illuminated Greek Manuscripts from American Collections: An Exhibition in Honor of Kurt Weitzmann,* ed. Gary Vikan (Princeton, 1973), no. 1, pp. 52ff.; fig. 1 and frontispiece.

4. A. M. Friend, Jr., "The Portraits of the Evangelists in Greek and Latin Manuscripts," part 1, *Art Studies* 5 (1927), p. 134 and pl. 8, figs. 95–98; part 2, *Art Studies* 7 (1929), pp. 11ff. and figs. 11, 12, 15, 16, 18, 37. Weitzmann, *Byzantinische Buchmalerei,* pp. 23ff. and pl. 30, figs. 169–72.

5. Friend, "Evangelists," part 1, p. 142 and pl. 16, figs. 156–57. K. Weitzmann, "Probleme der mittelbyzantinischen Renaissance," *Archaeologischer Anzeiger* (1933), p. 346 and figs. 5 and 7.

6. K. Weitzmann, "Geistige Grundlagen und Wesen der Makedonischen Renaissance," *Arbeitsgemeinschaft für Forschung des Landes Nordrhein-Westfalen,* fasc. 107 (Cologne and Opladen, 1963; reprinted in English, "The Character and Intellectual Origins of the Macedonian Renaissance," *Studies* (see note 1 above), p. 176ff., 199, and figs. 180–81.

Fig. 3. John. Princeton, University Library, cod. Garrett 6, fol. 130v

4. In fear that the classical model carried too far might impair the Christian character of Byzantine art, a reaction set in in the eleventh century that, without abandoning the formal classical repertory, introduced elements aspiring to greater spirituality. In the figures in a Lectionary on Mount Sinai, cod. 204, dating from the turn of the millennium, the artistic means to this goal were, first of all, a de-materialization of the human body through slender proportions and, as is seen in the figure of the evangelist Mark,[7] a slightly swaying pose. In another figure, that

7. V. Beneševič, *Monumenta Sinaitica*, fasc. 1 (Leningrad, 1925), p. 47 and pl. 27. Weitzmann, "Geistige Grundlagen," p. 49 and color plate 1. Figs. 5, 20–21, 33–34 are published through the courtesy of the Alexandria-Michigan-Princeton Expedition to Mount Sinai.

Fig. 4. Matthew. Mount Athos, Stauronikita, cod. 43, fol. 10r

of a certain holy monk Peter, dematerialization is achieved by a complete flattening of the garments, beneath which is hidden a frail, emaciated body (fig. 5).[8] Here the ideal of asceticism has found expression without reverting to the more abstract forms of the hieratic mode. By concentrating on the faces, which reveal great intellectual power, this sophisticated, highly aristocratic culture expresses a spiritual mode.

8. Beneševič, *Monumenta Sinaitica*, pl. 28. K. Weitzmann, "The Classical in Byzantine Art as a Mode of Individual Expression," *Byzantine Art: An European Art, Ninth Exhibition Held under the Auspices of the Council of Europe. Lectures* (Athens, 1966), pp. 165ff. (reprinted in *Studies*, p. 165 and fig. 144). Idem, *Illustrated Manuscripts at St. Catherine's Monastery on Mount Sinai*, Medieval and Renaissance Studies, the Monastic Microfilm Library, St. John's University (Collegeville, Minn., 1973), p. 14 and fig. 14.

Fig. 5. Peter of Monobata. Mount Sinai, cod. 204, fol. 3r

5. Byzantine art was able to represent dogmatic beliefs by concise pictorial means, and to incorporate them into the broader framework of a religious art in which the impact of the Divine Liturgy became so predominant that one can speak of Middle and Late Byzantine art as a liturgical art *par excellence*. Nothing could be more characteristic of the Byzantine mind than the fact that the Harrowing of Hell, which is not even canonical, was chosen as subject for the greatest feast of the Church, Easter Sunday, because it is a pictorial expression of the

Fig. 6. Anastasis. Mount Athos, Dionysiou, cod. 587, fol. 2r

dogma of the two natures of Christ, whereby his human nature was retained even after his death on the cross. In any Gospel Lectionary, as for example the splendid manuscript from the Dionysiou monastery on Mount Athos, this scene heads the first, that is, the Easter periscope (fig. 6).[9]

6. Belatedly, Byzantine art adopted emotionalism as a mode of expression; earlier it had been consciously avoided for fear of endangering the hieratic. But when finally employed, the Byzantines were able to use emotionalism very effectively to enhance the spiritual, at the same time withstanding the temptation to embark—as did the Latin West—on a road to earthly realism. In a New Testament and Psalter in Moscow, John, heading the Apocalypse (fig. 7),[10] is depicted in whirling, billowing garments, the pictorial expression of the inner turmoil that has shaken his frail body. The high emotional pitch of this composition, empha-

9. M. Beza, *Byzantine Art in Roumania* (London, 1940), fig. on p. 53; K. Weitzmann, "Byzantine Miniature and Icon Painting in the Eleventh Century," *Proceedings of the XIIIth International Congress of Byzantine Studies, Oxford, 1966* (London, 1967), p. 216 and pl. 24 (reprinted in *Studies*, p. 290 and fig. 286).

10. M. V. Alpatoff, "A Byzantine Illuminated Manuscript of the Palaeologue Epoch in Moscow," *Art Bulletin* 12 (1930), pp. 207ff. and fig. 3.

Fig. 7. John. Moscow, Historical Museum, cod. gr. 407, fol. 388v

sized by the fleeting highlights, anticipates in more than one respect the art of El Greco.

Let us now turn to our primary concern, the study of Byzantine book illumination, past, present, and future. The study in depth of any scholarly subject may be considered in terms of the ever-widening circles of ripples generated by a stone cast into a pond. The strong profile of the inner circles becomes less and less distinct in the outer ones. We have chosen for convenience the number of seven circles, without attaching to it the mystical connotation of an *hebdomas*.

The First Circle: Documentary Evidence

We shall deal briefly with the first circle, in which our concern is with the collection and publication of the documents. Here art history pursues three distinct approaches.

First, in the tradition of learned librarians who present their treasures in their custody in the form of catalogues,[11] art historians in like manner began to publish catalogues of only the illustrated manuscripts in a given collection. Most successful in this respect have been the publications of the National Library of Vienna, which in the days of the Hapsburg monarchy embarked on such a project on a lavish and unequaled scale.[12] But as long as no catalogues have been published of the illustrated manuscripts of the other large and most important collections, such as those in the Vatican, the Bibliothèque Nationale,[13] the British Museum, and the monasteries of Mounts Athos[14] and Sinai,[15] we still have not even approximate

---

11. One of the earliest catalogues reproducing illustrations in engravings, such as those of the Vienna Genesis, is that of the Vienna Nationalbibliothek: Petri Lambecii Hamburgensis, *Commentariorum de Augustissima Bibliotheca Caesarea Vindobonensi*, Liber III no. II (Vienna, 1670), pp. 2ff. and pls. 1–49.

12. *Beschreibendes Verzeichnis der Illuminierten Handschriften in Österreich*, edited successively by F. Wickhoff, M. Dvorák, J. von Schlosser and H. J. Hermann. Two volumes deal with the illustrated Greek manuscripts: P. Buberl, *Der Wiener Dioscurides und die Wiener Genesis* (Leipzig, 1937); P. Buberl and H. Gerstinger, *Die Handschriften des X.–XVIII. Jahrhunderts* (Leipzig, 1938).

13. H. Omont, *Miniatures des plus anciens manuscrits de la Bibliothèque Nationale du VIᵉ au XIVᵉ siècle*, 2d ed. (Paris, 1929), presents only a few selected important manuscripts.

14. The Patriarchal Foundation of Patristic Studies at Thessalonike, founded in 1968 under the aegis of the Patriarchate of Constantinople, has embarked on a project to publish the miniatures of all Athos monasteries; the first volume, including the illustrated manuscripts of the monastery of Dionysiou, has appeared. S. M. Pelekanides, P. C. Christou, C. Tsioumis, S. N. Kadas, *The Treasures of Mount Athos: Illuminated Manuscripts*, vol. 1, *The Protaton and the Monasteries of Dionysiou, Koutloumousiou, Xeropotamou and Gregoriou* (Athens, 1973).

15. A volume containing the illustrated manuscripts of Saint Catherine's monastery on Mount Sinai is contemplated by the author within the framework of the publications of the Alexandria-Michigan-Princeton expedition to Mount Sinai.

control over the vast material of Byzantine miniature painting.[16] Library catalogues have recently been supplemented by exhibition catalogues that originated as modest handlists[17] but in time became publications so rich in information that they have become indispensable tools of research.[18]

The second approach is to assemble all existing miniature cycles of a given text, thus laying the foundation for extensive comparative iconographical study. This method, first applied to Western miniature cycles such as those of the *Psychomachia* of Prudentius[19] and the Comedies of Terence,[20] was adopted by Rufus Morey and Albert Friend for their monumental enterprise of publishing all the illustrated manuscripts of the Septuagint, as the documentary basis for a comprehensive history of Bible illustration.[21]

Meanwhile, the comparative method has been applied to illustrated texts of smaller scope in the publication of all extant manuscripts of the *Heavenly Ladder* of John Climacus by John Rupert Martin,[22] and of the liturgical collection of sixteen homilies of Gregory of Nazianzus by George Galavaris.[23] A study of the manuscripts of the *Christian Topography* of Cosmas Indicopleustes is in preparation.[24]

16. There exists, however, a catalogue of the Greek illustrated manuscripts of the Ambrosiana in Milan; see M. L. Gengaro, F. Leoni, G. Villa, *Codici decorati e miniati dell'Ambrosiana: Ebraici e Greci* (Milan, 1957).

17. A typical example is the catalogue of the Byzantine exhibition in Paris in 1931, where the barest information is given for each manuscript: *Exposition Internationale d'Art Byzantin, 28 Mai–9 Juillet 1931* (Paris, 1931), pp. 171ff.

18. E.g., J. Porcher and M.-L. Concasty, *Byzance et la France Médiévale, Manuscrits à peintures du II*e *au XVI*e *siècle, Bibliothèque Nationale* (Paris, 1958); and *Illuminated Greek Manuscripts* (see note 3 above).

19. R. Stettiner, *Die Illustrierten Prudentiushandschriften* (Berlin, text 1895; plates 1905).

20. L. W. Jones and C. R. Morey, *The Miniatures of the Manuscripts of Terence* 2 vols. (Princeton, 1931).

21. So far only two volumes of unique Psalter manuscripts have appeared, both written by the late Ernest T. DeWald: *Vaticanus graecus 1927* and *Vaticanus graecus 752, The Illustrations in the Manuscripts of the Septuagint*, vol. 3, parts 1 and 2 (Princeton, 1941 and 1942). But these are not representative of the project as a whole, since they offer no chance to apply the comparative method. This method will, however, be employed in the next volume, which will contain the Octateuchs.

22. J. R. Martin, *The Illustrations of the Heavenly Ladder of John Climacus*, Studies in Manuscript Illumination, vol. 5 (Princeton, 1954).

23. G. Galavaris, *The Illustrations of the Liturgical Homilies of Gregory Nazianzenus*, Studies in Manuscript Illumination, vol. 6 (Princeton, 1969).

24. For a preliminary study, see D. Mouriki-Charalambous, "The Octateuch Miniatures of the Byzantine Manuscripts of Cosmas Indicopleustes" (Ph.D. diss., Department of Art and Archaeology, Princeton University, 1970).

For two other texts of the greatest importance, a comparative study of all existing miniature cycles has not yet been published. The first is the New Testament, for whose study Gabriel Millet laid the groundwork,[25] distinguishing two different recensions, one Alexandrian and the other Antiochian.[26] Yet we are still far from having a full and coherent study of the extant New Testament cycles. The second project, equally extensive and important, and waiting to be undertaken, is the comprehensive study of the illustrated Lives of Saints, supplementing the textual studies of the Bollandistes.

The third approach is the investigation of manuscripts by scriptoria, a task that demands the cooperation of historians, philologists, palaeographers, art historians, and codicologists alike. The tool of the art historian is stylistic criticism as it developed chiefly in Germany at the turn of the century. Under the inspiration and guidance of Adolph Goldschmidt, such studies were pursued for the Latin West, where the production of major scriptoria such as those of Saint Gall, Regensburg, Salzburg, Fulda, and Winchester, and later of Tours and Cologne, among others, could be traced with remarkable accuracy.[27] In this kind of stylistic grouping, the study of Byzantine manuscripts lags far behind, partly because of their lesser diversity in style. Constantinople, especially after the end of Iconoclasm, played such a dominant role that the issue, at least at the present state of our knowledge, is more or less confined to the question of what was produced in the capital and what in the provinces. A first attempt to define works of one of the major scriptoria of Constantinople, that of the Studios, by script, ornament, and illustration, was made recently by Eleopoulos.[28] More than a generation ago I wrote a study of ninth- and tenth-century Byzantine book illumination in

25. G. Millet, *Recherches sur l'Iconographie de l'Evangile* (Paris, 1916).

26. Millet's distinction of two different recensions has been challenged by S. Tsuji, "The Study of the Byzantine Gospel Illustrations in Florence, Laur. Plut. VI, 23 and Paris, Bibl. Nat. Cod. gr. 74" (Ph.D. diss., Department of Art and Archaeology, Princeton University, 1967). For the complete publication of the miniatures of these two codices, see H. Omont, *Evangiles avec peintures byzantines du XIᵉ siècle*, 2 vols. (Paris, n.d.); T. Velmans, *Le Tétraévangile de la Laurentienne, Florence, Laur. VI, 23* (Paris, 1971).

27. For the scriptorium of Saint Gall, see A. Merton, *Die Buchmalerei in St. Gallen* (Leipzig, 1912); for Regensburg, see G. Swarzenski, *Die Regensburger Buchmalerei des X. und XI. Jahrhunderts* (Leipzig, 1901); for Salzburg, see G. Swarzenski, *Die Salzburger Malerei von den ersten Anfängen bis zur Blütezeit des romanischen Stils* (Leipzig, 1908–1913); for Fulda, see H. Zimmerman, *Die Fuldaer Buchmalerei in Karolingischer und Ottonischer Zeit* (Vienna, 1911); for Winchester, see O. Homburger, *Die Anfänge der Malschule von Winchester im X. Jahrhundert* (Leipzig, 1912); for Tours, see W. Koehler, *Die karolingischen Miniaturen* (Berlin, 1930; reprinted 1963); for Cologne, see P. Bloch and H. Schnitzler, *Die Ottonische Kölner Malerschule*, 2 vols. (Düsseldorf, 1967 and 1970).

28. N. X. Eleopoulos, Ἡ Βιβλιοθήκη καὶ τὸ Βιβλιογραφικὸν ἐργαστήριον τῆς Μονῆς τῶν Στουδίου (Athens, 1967).

which I attempted to separate the Constantinopolitan schools from those of various provincial centers in Asia Minor, Palestine, southern Italy, and elsewhere.[29] Today I see that this attempt was in some respects premature and that some attributions must be reconsidered. Yet it may be hoped that, in spite of the peculiar difficulties inherent in the Byzantine material, other scholars might follow suit and write corresponding volumes for the subsequent centuries.[30]

From the aforesaid it must have become obvious that the time has not yet come for a comprehensive history of Byzantine book illumination. Such a history can only be written when one is exploring an entirely new field or when sufficient preliminary studies are available. The first to dare to write such an exploratory study, almost a century ago in 1876, was Nikodim Kondakoff.[31] It was truly a pioneering work, by the scholar who founded the discipline of Byzantine art history as we know it today and who had an astonishing command of the manuscript material of Western as well as Eastern libraries. It is to be hoped that a second Kondakoff will some day write a more comprehensive history, as competent as the first was in its time.

The Second Circle: Reconstruction of Fragmentary Manuscripts

Even when all the surviving illustrated Byzantine manuscripts have been published in documentary fashion, we still will not have a basis broad enough to write an intelligent history of the subject. Actually, any history that confines itself to extant material is a falsification, since the preserved material is only a fraction of what once existed, and its survival is due merely to chance. It must therefore be the aim of the historian to adduce all tangible evidence that will contribute to a broader picture, even at the risk of making occasional mistakes which, however, are less damaging than a history distorted by too restricted evidence—and this leads us into the second circle. Here one can learn from the classical archaeologist, who from fragmentary remains proposes reconstructions of temple pediments like those of Aegina, Olympia, the Parthenon, and even Epidaurus, from which so little is left.

By a similar method we must reconstruct the fragments of some of our most precious Early Byzantine manuscripts. The sixth-century Vienna Genesis today contains only twenty-four purple leaves, the lower half of each, recto and verso, occupied by a miniature. The reconstruction of the gatherings by Paul Buberl shows that the manuscript originally possessed ninety-six folios, that is, one hundred ninety-two pages and consequently as many miniatures.[32] Moreover, it

29. See note 3 above.

30. For the Palaeologan period a hopeful beginning with regard to some scriptoria in Constantinople has been made by Hugo Buchthal in this volume.

31. N. P. Kondakoff, *Histoire de l'Art Byzantin, considéré principalement dans les miniatures*, 2 vols., translated from the Russian by M. Trawinski (Paris, 1886 and 1891).

32. Buberl, *Die Byzantinischen Handschriften*, vol. 1, pp. 77ff.

must be realized that each miniature contains two or three scenes, such as the miniature in which Abraham is promised posterity as numerous as the stars, then returns to his servants, and finally is informed about the posterity of his brother Nahor (fig. 8).[33] This would indicate a cycle of at least four hundred and perhaps as many as five hundred iconographical units. The Vienna Genesis is a deluxe manuscript and, as happened repeatedly in the case of such showpieces, the text is abbreviated to allow for the extravagant display of pictures; so in the third scene of this miniature, the corresponding verses have been omitted. Surely the model must have had a full text with each scene related to the proper passage. What such a model must have looked like is suggested in the reconstruction drawing (fig. 9).[34] Here picture and text are related in a manner typical of extensive narrative cycles.

Nor is the Vienna Genesis unique as a richly illustrated Book of Genesis. A second, equally famous and of the sixth century, was once in the possession of Sir Robert Cotton and is therefore called the Cotton Genesis.[35] It attracted one of the greatest scholars of his time, Peiresc, who had it lent to him in France in 1618 in order to publish a facsimile with engravings, which, however, never materialized. Only two preliminary drawings survive from this project, one of them depicting the Third Day of Creation (fig. 10).[36] These drawings are all the more valuable since the manuscript, after it was given to the British Museum, burned in 1731. There survive only charred fragments, like that used for the reconstruction drawing (fig. 11).[37] Originally the manuscript had as many as 330 miniatures.[38]

33. Gerstinger, *Wiener Genesis*, p. 84 and *pictura* 11. Buberl, *Die Byzantinischen Handschriften*, vol. 1, p. 94 and pl. 26, *pictura* 11.

34. K. Weitzmann, *Illustrations in Roll and Codex: A Study of the Origin and Method of Text Illustration*, Studies in Manuscript Illumination, vol. 2, 2d ed. (Princeton, 1970), p. 89, text figure D and pl. 27, fig. 73. Idem, "Illustration of the Septuagint," *Studies*, p. 52 and fig. 30.

35. *Vetusta Monumenta Rerum Brittannicarum*, vol. 1 (London, 1747), pls. 66–68. F. W. Gotch, *A Supplement to Tischendorf's Reliquiae ex incendio ereptae codicis celeberrimi Cottoniani* (London, 1881).

36. H. Omont, "Fragments du manuscrit de la Genèse de R. Cotton, conservés parmi les papiers de Peiresc," in *Mémoires de la Société Nationale des Antiquaires de France* 53, pp. 163ff. and 2 pls. Idem, *Miniatures*, Introduction, pp. 1ff. and plate.

37. K. Weitzmann, "Observations on the Cotton Genesis Fragments," *Late Classical and Mediaeval Studies in Honor of Albert Mathias Friend, Jr.* (Princeton, 1955), pp. 112ff., pl. 14 figs. 3–4 and text figure A. For the reconstruction drawings in general, see Sahoko Tsuji, "La Chaire de Maximien, la Genèse de Cotton et les mosaiques de Saint-Marc à Venise: à propos du cycle de Joseph," *Synthronon: Recueil d'études dédié au Prof. A. Grabar* (Paris, 1968), pp. 43ff.; idem, "Un Essai d'identification des sujets des miniatures fragmentaires de la Genèse de Cotton," *Journal of the Japan Art History Society* 17 (1967), pp. 35ff. (in Japanese); idem, "Nouvelles Observations sur les miniatures fragmentaires de la Genèse de Cotton: cycles de Lot, d'Abraham et de Jacob," *Cahiers Archéologiques* 20 (1970), pp. 29ff.

38. Weitzmann, "Observations," pp. 114ff.

Fig. 8. Story of Abraham. Vienna, Nationalbibliothek, cod. theol. gr. 31, *pictura* 11 (after Buberl)

Fig. 9. Reconstruction of the model
of the Vienna Genesis

Fig. 10. Third Day of Creation. Paris, Bibliothèque Nationale, cod. fr. 9530, fol. 32 (after Omont)

Fig. 11. Reconstruction of
Cotton Genesis miniature.
London, British Museum,
cod. Cotton Otho B.VI,
fol. 1r

Reconstructions of this kind, more than mere archaeological exercises, have far-reaching implications. Their importance is twofold. For the history of book art in general, these early fragments imply that Early Christian illumination was not a timid beginning of greater things to come, but a fully developed art, hardly to be surpassed at any later period. Never again was the Book of Genesis illustrated so extensively, and the same might be deduced for other books of the Bible that unfortunately have not been preserved.

The second implication concerns the origin of Christian art in general. Contrary to the general concept that it began in the catacombs as a symbolic art with few abbreviated scenes, gradually increasing in scope and number and developing into narrative art, early Bible illustration suggests that an extensive narrative art existed from the very beginning, side by side with funerary art, which was iconographically more restricted.

The Third Circle: Migration of Miniatures into Other Texts

In the third circle our concern turns to expanding knowledge within the limits of illustrated Byzantine manuscripts. Intensive occupation with miniature cycles of all kinds has led to the observation that quite often a picture does not fit the text it accompanies, but is much better explained by another text. From this fact can be deduced that the miniature was invented for the one text, which one might term the "basic text," and then taken over into the other. Figuratively, one may speak of the migration of miniatures.[39]

A good example, abounding with miniatures taken over from quite a number of different sources, is the monastic or marginal Psalter, of which the Chloudov Psalter in the Historical Museum of Moscow, datable in the ninth century, is one of the earliest, richest, and artistically most distinct.[40] Verses 17 and 23 of Psalm 105, "He sent a man before them, even Joseph, who was sold for a servant," and "Israel also came into Egypt and Jacob sojourned in the land of Ham," are obviously not sufficient explanation for the marginal scenes (fig. 12). The first of these shows little Joseph being sold to the Ishmaelite merchants, who then—in an obviously abbreviated scene—depart with a burdened camel; and the second depicts the arrival of Jacob in Egypt with his family on an oxcart, being announced to the enthroned Joseph by a messenger. Such detailed narrative was obviously taken over from an illustrated Book of Genesis and thus, iconographically speaking, it belongs primarily to the history of Genesis illustration and only secondarily to that of the Psalter.

---

39. Weitzmann, *Roll and Codex*, 2d ed., pp. 134ff.

40. N. P. Kondakoff, *Minjature Greceskoj rukopisi Psaltiri IX beka iz Sobranija A. N. Chludova* (Moscow, 1878). A facsimile by Mrs. Tchepkina, curator of manuscripts of the Historical Museum, is awaited. For Greek Psalter illustration in general, see J. J. Tikkanen, *Die Psalterillustration im Mittelalter*, Acta Societatis Scientiarum Fennicae vol. 31, no. 5 (Helsingfors, 1903).

An analogous and even more conspicuous case is the extensive Joseph cycle, which in the well-known Gregory of Nazianzus manuscript in Paris, dating from the end of the ninth century, precedes the homily "In Defense of his Flight to Pontus" (fig. 13).[41] This cycle is explained neither by this nor any other of Gregory's homilies and the reason for its inclusion in this manuscript remains a mystery.[42] On the other hand, there can be no doubt that such a cycle must have been copied from an illustrated Book of Genesis, including perhaps elements from an apocryphal Joseph legend. Most likely the cycle of the model was not copied in its entirety, but was epitomized for this Gregory miniature. Obviously, then, these illustrations must also be treated primarily as Genesis illustrations.

Two observations have a bearing on the history of these epitomized Joseph cycles. First, it will be noticed that the Ishmaelite merchants in both the Psalter and the Paris Gregory manuscripts are dressed in Persian costume, and from this and other details it may be deduced that the Joseph scenes of both manuscripts belong to the same pictorial recension. Secondly, comparison with the other established pictorial recensions, those of the Vienna and the Cotton Genesis, leads to the conclusion that the scenes from the Psalter and the Gregory agree with none of them and that consequently there must have existed a third recension that we can trace only through migrated miniatures.[43]

The Chloudov Psalter and the Paris Gregory represent a type of illustrated manuscript that one might call "polycyclic," that is, they contain miniatures excerpted from a variety of sources.[44] Among the polycyclic manuscripts, a unique position is taken by the ninth-century codex of the Sacra Parallela in Paris, cod. gr. 923, because it has, as is the nature of a *florilegium*, neither an original text nor original pictures.[45] Whatever illustrations it has, and they are to be counted by the hundreds, were made for the original texts, and when they were cut up and selected passages chosen for the *florilegium*, the pictures went along. There are, for example, several scenes from the Book of Job, one of them (fig. 14) illustrating the Slaying of Job's Children according to verse 19 of chapter 1: "And behold, there came a great wind from the wilderness, and smote the four corners of

41. Omont, *Miniatures*, pl. 26.

42. S. Der Nersessian, "The Illustrations of the Homilies of Gregory of Nazianzus, Paris gr. 510: A Study of the Connections between Text and Images," *Dumbarton Oaks Papers* 16 (1962), p. 223 and pl. 18.

43. There is yet another recension of Genesis illustrations, a fourth, which forms part of the Octateuchs; see Weitzmann, "Illustration of the Septuagint," *Studies*, pp. 52ff.

44. Weitzmann, *Roll and Codex*, 2d ed., pp. 196ff.

45. J. Rendel Harris, *Fragments of Philo Judaeus* (Cambridge, 1886). Weitzmann, *Byzantinische Buchmalerei*, p. 80 and pl. 86. Idem, "Illustration of the Septuagint," *Studies*, pp. 56f., 62f., and figs. 35–36, 41, 43–44. A. Grabar, *Les Manuscrits grecs enluminés de provenance italienne* (Paris, 1972), pp. 21ff., pls. 6–11. A full publication of the miniatures is being prepared by the author.

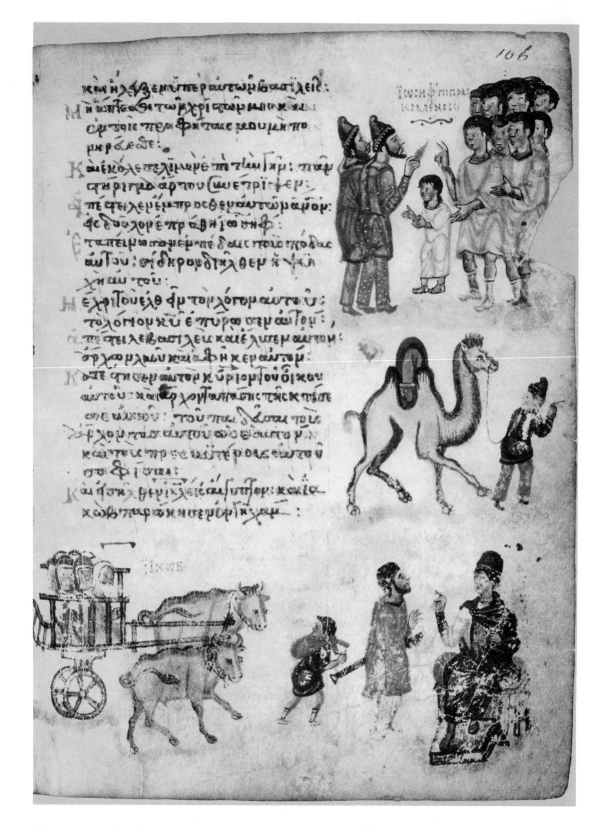

Fig. 12. Story of Joseph. Moscow, Historical Museum, cod. gr. 129, fol. 160r

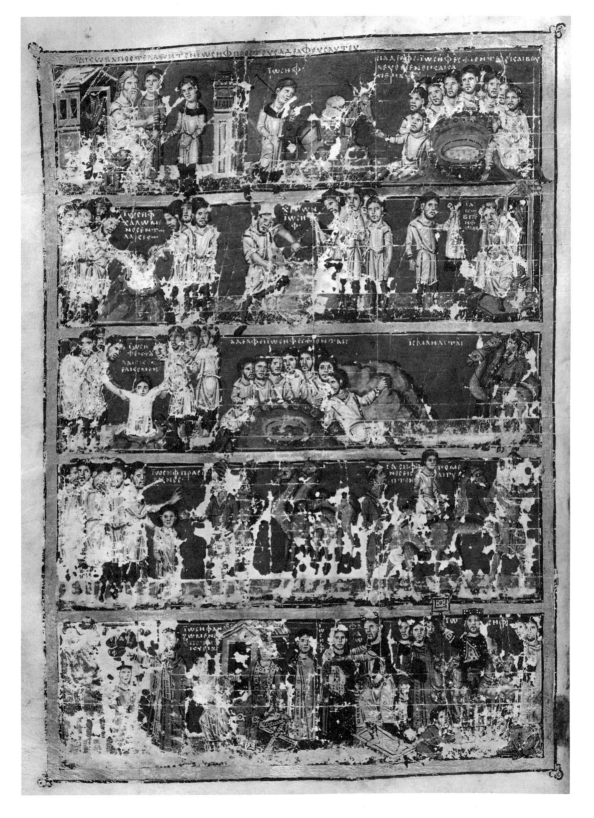

Fig. 13. Story of Joseph. Paris, Bibliothèque Nationale, cod. gr. 510, fol. 69v

20

Fig. 14. Slaying of Job's Children.
Paris, Bibliothèque Nationale,
cod. gr. 923, fol. 204v

Fig. 15. Slaying of Job's Children.
Rome, Vatican Library,
cod. gr. 749, fol. 20r

the house, and it fell upon the young men and they are dead." The winds are pictorialized by trumpet-blowing devils, this same motif occurring in a miniature of a ninth-century Job manuscript in the Vatican Library (fig. 15),[46] which is very closely related in other details as well, proving that the Sacra Parallela miniature was indeed taken over from a Job manuscript.

In a similar manner scenes were taken over into the Sacra Parallela from illustrated Books of Genesis, Kings, the Gospels, the Acts of the Apostles, and several other texts. Striking examples are the illustrations at the beginning of Acts 5 (fig. 16), where we see Ananias first facing Peter and John and then falling dead at their feet. This conflated scene is followed immediately by the removal of the corpse for burial. On the next page is depicted the identical fate of his wife, Sapphira, in an equally dramatic sequence. The first of these four scenes, in the same conflated form, occurs also—here in its original context—in the illustrated Acts of the Rockefeller McCormick New Testament, a thirteenth-century codex in the library of the University of Chicago (fig. 17).[47] But it is only on the basis of the migrated miniatures in the Sacra Parallela that we can be sure of an early illustrated Book of Acts that must have had a sequence of such density that it rivaled the most prolifically illustrated Gospel books.[48]

Moreover, the importance of the Sacra Parallela manuscript is greatly enhanced by the fact that it contains miniatures from certain books of the Septuagint, such as the *Sapientia Solomonis*, of which no copy has survived.[49] The same holds true for scenes from certain patristic texts and even such books as Flavius Josephus' *Antiquitates Judaicae* and *Bellum Judaicum*.[50]

There are other polycyclic manuscripts, such as the Cosmas Indicopleustes and the Gospel Lectionary, whose miniatures must be grouped according to the basic texts from which the pictures were taken. This process of disentanglement, while not increasing the documentary knowledge, nevertheless greatly adds to our

46. Weitzmann, *Byzantinische Buchmalerei*, pp. 77ff. and pls. 83–85; Grabar, *Manuscrits*, pp. 16ff. and pls. 1–3.

47. H. R. Willoughby, *The Rockefeller McCormick New Testament* (Chicago, 1932), vol. 3, p. 248ff. and vol. 1, pl. fol. 111r; *Illuminated Greek Manuscripts*, no. 45, pp. 162ff.

48. For a discussion of the problem of narrative illustration in Acts, see H. L. Kessler, "Paris Gr. 102: A Rare Illustrated Acts of the Apostles," *Dumbarton Oaks Papers* 27 (1973), pp. 209–16.

49. Weitzmann, "Illustration of the Septuagint," *Studies*, p. 63 and fig. 41.

50. Weitzmann, *Roll and Codex*, 2d ed., p. 134 and pl. 36, fig. 115. Idem, "Zur Frage des Einflusses jüdischer Bilderquellen auf die Illustration des Alten Testamentes," *Mullus: Festschrift Theodor Klauser. Jahrbuch für Antike und Christentum*, supplement, vol. 1 (Münster, 1964), pp. 406, 409–11, 413–15 (reprinted in English: "The Question of the Influence of Jewish Pictorial Sources on Old Testament Illustration," *Studies*, pp. 84, 88–90, 93–95).

Fig. 16a–b. Story of Ananias and Sapphira. Paris, Bibliothèque Nationale, cod. gr. 923, fols. 314r–v

knowledge of many illustrated texts with prolific miniature cycles that once must have existed and that today survive only as migrated stray miniatures.

The Fourth Circle: Copying in Other Media

Within the next, our fourth circle, we move out of the realm of miniatures into other media that, we should like to demonstrate, depend on illustrated manuscripts for their sources. Here again we employ a method familiar to classical archaeologists, who as a matter of course discuss lost Greek bronze statues on the basis of their Roman marble copies, or the lost frescoes of Polygnotos on the basis of vase paintings.

Ever since the Finnish scholar Tikkanen proved in 1889 that the Cotton Genesis or a related copy served as model for the mosaics in the narthex of San

Fig. 17. Story of Ananias. Chicago, University Library, cod. 965, fol. 111r

Marco in Venice,[51] his discovery has been cited as the chief paradigm demonstrating that monumental narrative cycles of this kind are dependent on book illumination.[52] In this case the mosaicists have followed their manuscript model, which I believe to have been the Cotton Genesis itself, very closely indeed, but one must take into consideration certain guiding principles in order to understand such a copying process. Rich as the Genesis cycle of San Marco is, spreading over five cupolas, two broad arches, lunettes, and spandrels, the mosaicist could accommo-

51. J. J. Tikkanen, *Die Genesismosaiken von S. Marco in Venedig und ihr Verhältniss zu den Miniaturen der Cottonbibel*, *Acta Societatis Scientiarum Fennicae*, vol. 17 (Helsingfors, 1889), pp. 99ff.

52. Weitzmann, "Observations," pp. 119ff. See also Kitzinger, "The Role of Miniature Painting in Mural Decoration," in the present volume.

date only about one hundred scenes from the more than three hundred in the manuscript. Thus one inevitably encounters epitomes, and in other instances, where narrative cycles such as the mosaics of Santa Maria Maggiore[53] and the frescoes of Old Saint Peter's and of San Paolo in Rome are spread over church walls, this process of epitomization went even further.

Furthermore, the mosaicist must be more economical with space than the miniaturist. In the second preserved watercolor, where the illustrator of the Cotton Genesis depicts Abraham speaking to the Lord (fig. 18), the figure of the patriarch moves freely in space, facing the enormous hand of God, which issues from a huge segment of sky.[54] In the mosaic (fig. 19), the allotted picture area for the parallel representation is limited to the width of the figure of Abraham, and the shrunken segment of sky, to save space, is located above the figures of the preceding scene.[55]

While the relationship between monumental painting and book illumination has been discussed repeatedly and at length, a new medium—icon painting—which sheds new light on this problem, has only recently been introduced.[56] Here the similarities with book illumination are even greater, since evidence is accumulating that in many instances miniaturist and icon painter were the same person. There is, for example, at Sinai a previously unpublished huge icon of Moses Receiving the Law (fig. 20), dating from the turn of the twelfth to the thirteenth century and unfortunately not yet fully cleaned, on whose frame are depicted twenty scenes from the life of Moses, from his birth at the upper left to his death at the lower right. His birth is rendered according to a convention used for the birth of Christ, the Virgin, or John the Baptist, and this immediately reveals dependence on the twelfth-century Octateuchs where, at the beginning of Exodus, the same composition has been adapted.[57] After the birth of the infant Moses and his rescue from the Nile, there follow two apocryphal scenes (fig. 21), which are fully explained by a passage in the *Antiquitates Judaicae* of Flavius Josephus (II.IX.7). According to this story, Pharaoh's daughter, here named Thermuthis,

53. For the relationship between mosaic and miniature in this particular case, see Kitzinger, "The Role of Miniature Painting."

54. Omont, "Fragments," pp. 163ff. and plate. Idem, *Miniatures*, Introduction, pp. 1ff. and plate.

55. O. Demus, *Die Mosaiken von San Marco in Venedig* (Vienna, 1935), p. 62 and pl. 28. Weitzmann, "Narrations in Early Christendom," *American Journal of Archaeology* 61 (1957), pp. 88ff. and pl. 35, figs. 10–11.

56. Most important in this connection is the icon collection in Saint Catherine's monastery on Mount Sinai; see G. and M. Sotiriou, *Icones du Mont Sinai*, 2 vols. (Athens, 1956 and 1958).

57. E.g., the Octateuch of Smyrna. D.-C. Hesseling, *Miniatures de l'Octateuch grec de Smyrne* (Leiden, 1909), p. 50, fig. 152. Weitzmann, "The Octateuch of the Seraglio and the History of its Picture Recension," *Actes du X. congrès international d'études byzantines* (Istanbul, 1957), pp. 173ff. and pl. 41, figs. 5–6.

Fig. 18. Abraham. Paris, Bibliothèque Nationale, cod. fr. 9530, fol. 31 (after Omont)

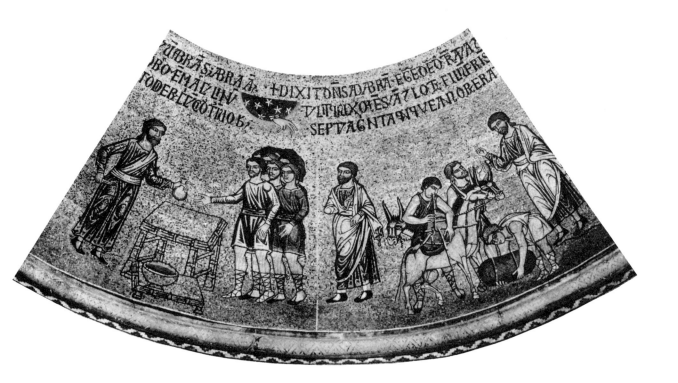

Fig. 19. Abraham. Venice, San Marco. Mosaic

26

Fig. 20. Moses Receiving the Law. Mount Sinai. Icon

Fig. 21a–b. Scenes from Moses' Infancy.
Mount Sinai. Icon (details)

Fig. 22. Moses' Infancy.
Rome, Vatican Library,
cod. gr. 746, fol. 153r

leads the little Moses to Pharaoh, hoping that he would make the boy his successor. The first scene is a literal illustration of the passage "and Pharaoh took him to his breast . . . [and] . . . embraced him lovingly." Moses, so the story goes, in sheer childishness threw the diadem given him by Pharaoh to the ground, thus incurring his wrath and intention to kill him. But Thermuthis forestalled Pharaoh and "snatched the child away," as is literally depicted in the second scene. In the Octateuchs this episode is likewise interpolated (fig. 22),[58] though an earlier phase was chosen, depicting the child Moses running eagerly toward Pharaoh. Presumably in the common model there appeared all three phases of the story, of which the first is preserved in the Vatican Octateuch cod. gr. 746 and the other two in the icon frame.

The Moses icon is rather unique; we know of no other in existence whose frame is filled with an Old Testament narrative cycle. We expect to make the greatest gain from the study of narrative icon frames depicting the lives of saints. Icons from the Sinai monastery[59] depicting Saints Nicholas, George, Catherine, and others display on their frames epitomized cycles with from sixteen to twenty scenes each, apparently derived from miniature cycles, while in the extant menologia only very few stray miniatures have survived.

The influence of miniatures extends beyond monumental and icon painting to a variety of media within the so-called applied arts. For instance, the eleventh-century carvers of an extensive ivory cycle of Creation scenes, once mounted on an antependium in the cathedral of Salerno (fig. 23),[60] employed as model a manuscript that must have belonged to the Cotton Genesis recension.[61] This is clearly indicated by their most characteristic common feature, the Creator in human form (cf. figs. 10 and 11), in places where other recensions show only the hand of God. The angels—or rather the personifications of the days—standing in front of the Creator in the Cotton Genesis miniature, are placed behind him in the ivory. This example of the dependence of ivories on miniatures is by no means unique. A few scenes from the Vienna Genesis were copied on the plaques of a tenth-century Byzantine rosette casket,[62] and the tenth-century Joshua Rotulus, almost as soon as it was created, became so famous that ivory carvers copied several of its scenes for the decoration of another casket.[63]

58. Weitzmann, "Jüdische Bilderquellen," p. 406 and pl. 15b (reprinted in *Studies*, p. 85 and fig. 63).

59. Sotiriou, *Icones*, vol. 1, figs. 165–67; 169–70; vol. 2, 144ff., 154ff.

60. A. Goldschmidt, *Die Elfenbeinskulpturen*, vol. 4 (Berlin, 1926), pp. 36ff. and pls. 42–48. A. Carucci, *Gli avori salernitani del sec. XII. Iconografia* (Salerno, 1965).

61. Weitzmann, "Observations," pp. 122ff. see also R. Bergman, "The Salerno Ivories" (Ph.D. diss., Department of Art and Archaeology, Princeton University, 1972).

62. A. Goldschmidt and K. Weitzmann, *Die Byzantinischen Elfenbeinskulpturen des X.–XIII. Jahrhunderts*, vol. 1 (Berlin, 1930), p. 28, nos. 13–15, and pl. 7.

63. Ibid., p. 23f., nos. 1–4 and pl. 1. The relationship between other ivory caskets with rich cycles from the David and Joseph stories and their miniature models remains

Fig. 23. Creation scenes. Salerno, Cathedral. Ivory

If similar relationships between miniatures and metalwork cannot be demon-strated in such detail, we must blame the greater destructibility of metal. Yet there is one important set of silver plates with the story of David in the Metropoli-tan Museum of Art in New York and the Museum of Nicosia at Cyprus about which Dalton, the first to publish them in 1900, significantly remarked, "the real importance of the series lies in its relation to the illuminated Byzantine Psalters."[64] In the study of the Paris Psalter by Hugo Buchthal, the close relation of some of its miniatures, especially the one of the fight between David and Goliath (fig. 24) with the silver plate that exceeds all others in size and complexity (fig. 25),[65] has been fully recognized, although a more complete investigation of this relationship, taking into account the full evidence provided by Byzantine Psalter miniatures, has yet to be made.[66] What makes this study so important is the fact

---

to be investigated; ibid., p. 63f., no. 123 and pls. 70–71 (Palazzo di Venezia, Rome) and p. 64, no. 124 and pls. 71–75 (Sens, Cathedral).

64. O. M. Dalton, "A Second Silver Treasure from the District of Kyrenia, Cyprus," *Archaeologia* 57 (1900), pp. 159ff. Idem, "Byzantine Plate and Jewelry from Cyprus in Mr. Morgan's Collection," *Burlington Magazine* 10 (1906–1907), pp. 355ff.

65. H. Buchthal, *The Miniatures of the Paris Psalter* (London, 1938), pp. 21ff., pl. 4 and pl. 21, fig. 44.

66. K. Weitzmann, "Prolegomena to a Study of the Cyprus plates," *Metropolitan Museum Journal* 3 (1970), pp. 97ff.

Kurt Weitzmann

Fig. 24. David and Goliath. Paris, Bibliothèque Nationale, cod. gr. 139, fol. 4v

that the silver plates, from the time of the emperor Heraclius (610–641), antedate by about three centuries the Paris Psalter, the earliest copy of the so-called aristocratic recension. It is, thus, hardly surprising that in some respects the plates reflect the lost miniature archetype better than any of the extant miniatures.

We shall not attempt here to enumerate all the media for which, on occasion, miniature cycles served as inspiration. Reflections can be found in marble and wooden sculpture, in gold, silver, and bronze reliefs, and in many other media, including even textiles, which are basically unsuitable for narrative illustration. Their study is fruitful from various points of view: they fill gaps within established

Fig. 25. David and Goliath. New York, Metropolitan Museum of Art. Silver plate

cycles, lead us on occasion closer to the archetypal representations, and in some
cases preserve remnants of otherwise totally lost miniature recensions.

The Fifth Circle: Impact on Other Cultures

Our fifth circle is concerned with the impact of Byzantine book illumination on
countries outside the empire. Here one must distinguish clearly between pre- and
post-Iconoclastic art. When Constantinople first began to build up an artistic

tradition of its own, it was in competition with the older metropolitan centers, Alexandria, Antioch, and Rome, each of which had a style of its own although these styles were more or less variants of a Christian *koïne*. This changed after the end of Iconoclasm when the Macedonian emperors established Constantinople as the arbiter of all artistic matters within and beyond the Christian world. The dissemination of Byzantine art into the Eastern Christian and Arab world, into the Slavic countries, and into Western Europe can only be compared with the expansion of Hellenistic art in the wake of Alexander's conquests.

In post-Iconoclastic book illumination the most characteristic representative of a largely liturgy-oriented art was the Gospel Lectionary because of its placement on the altar table and its important role in the service. Its decoration crystallizes in the pictures of great feasts, and it was these that most strongly attracted other Christian countries.

The Coptic church's own very strong artistic tradition is evident in the miniature cycle of the richest illustrated Coptic manuscript known, a Gospel book in Paris, Bibliothèque Nationale copte 13, written between A.D. 1178 and 1180 by the metropolitan Michael of Damietta.[67] In its miniature cycle, native Coptic elements, chiefly evident in the plain narrative illustrations, can be distinguished from later Byzantine intrusions. This distinction can be demonstrated in a single miniature such as the Washing of the Feet (fig. 26), where Christ, in accordance with Coptic liturgical practice, is seated while washing Peter's feet.[68] At the same time, we see one apostle loosening his sandals, a type invented during the Macedonian Renaissance in tenth-century Constantinople, where we find it first in an ivory in Berlin (fig. 27),[69] surely copied from a luxurious Lectionary miniature.[70] In this manner native Coptic and imported Byzantine elements are successfully combined.

Syrian art as a whole was more open to the influence of Constantinople than Coptic art, and more frequently copied its feast pictures intact rather than adopting details into its own tradition. One of the most forceful creations of the Macedonian Renaissance was a new Anastasis picture for Easter Sunday, well represented in a miniature of the so-called Phocas Lectionary in the Treasury of the Athos

67. M. Cramer, *Koptische Buchmalerei* (Recklinghausen, 1964), pp. 93ff. and figs. 70, 114, 120, 125, 129, 133, 135–36, 143 and pls. 14, 16–18. S. Shenouda, "The Miniatures of the Paris Manuscript Copte 13" (Ph.D. diss., Department of Art and Archaeology, Princeton University, 1956).

68. Shenouda, p. 189 and fig. 76.

69. Goldschmidt and Weitzmann, *Byzantinischen Elfenbeinskulpturen*, vol. 2 (Berlin, 1934), p. 28, no. 13, and pl. 4.

70. K. Weitzmann, "Ivory Sculpture of the Macedonian Renaissance," *Kolloquium über Spätantike und Frühmittelalterliche Skulptur*, vol. 2 (Mainz, 1970), p. 2 and pl. 2. Idem, "A 10th Century Lectionary: A Lost Masterpiece of the Macedonian Renaissance," *Revue des études sud-est européennes* 9 (1971), p. 626 and fig. 7.

Fig. 26. Washing of the Feet. Paris, Bibliothèque Nationale, cod. copt. 13, fol. 259v

Fig. 27. Washing of the Feet.
Berlin, Staatliche Museen. Ivory

Fig. 28.   Anastasis. Mount Athos, Lavra, Skevophylakion. Lectionary,
fol. 1v

monastery, Lavra (fig. 28).[71] This new type shows Christ dragging Adam out
of the Lower World just as Heracles had dragged Cerberus out of Hades.[72]
A Syriac Lectionary in the British Museum from around A.D. 1220 (fig. 29)
copies such a Byzantine model in every detail, with Christ stepping over the
crossed doors of Hades, Eve at the left above the kneeling Adam, and John the
Baptist above David and Solomon at the right.[73]

71. K. Weitzmann, "Das Evangelion im Skevophylakion zu Lawra," *Seminarium
Kondakovianum* 8 (1936), p. 87 and pl. 2, fig. 1. Idem, *Studies*, p. 210 and figs. 194–95.

72. Cf. the sarcophagus in the British Museum, London. Idem, "Skevophylakion,"
p. 88.

73. J. Leroy, *Les Manuscrits Syriaques à Peintures* (Paris, 1964), p. 308 and pl. 92,
fig. 1. F. R. Hosking, "The Manuscripts of Christian Asia," *The Book Through Five
Thousand Years* (London and New York, 1972), p. 106 and fig. 55 (color).

Fig. 29. Anastasis. London, British Museum, cod. add. 7170, fol. 156v

Georgian book illumination is at certain periods just as close if not closer to Constantinopolitan models, as may be demonstrated by an example from a twelfth-century Gospel book from Jruchi that has more than three hundred miniatures and, in this respect, rivals the richest extant Constantinopolitan Gospel books. One page with scenes from the Passion (fig. 30), the Deposition from the Cross, the Bewailing, the Anastasis with our Heracles-like Christ, and the Women at the Tomb, is a striking example of how very closely, even in small iconographical details, and with what good understanding of style, Georgian miniaturists were able to copy Constantinopolitan models.[74] This Gospel book—not the only one with such a rich cycle—makes obvious that any history of Byzantine New Testament illustration would be incomplete without including the richly illustrated Georgian Gospels.

74. H. Machavariani, *Georgian Manuscripts* (Tbilisi, 1970), p. 41 and pl. 33.

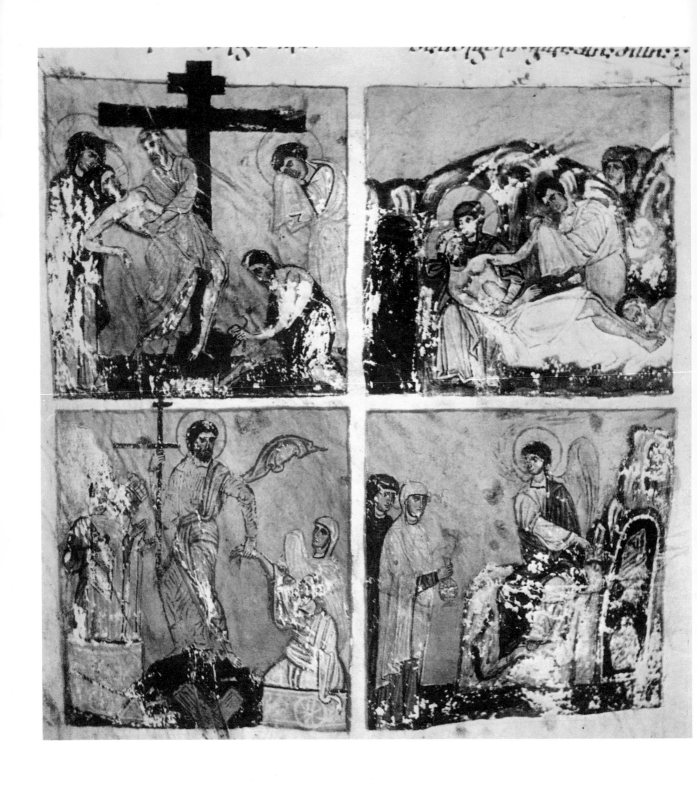

Fig. 30. Four Passion scenes. Tbilisi (Georgian S.S.R.), Academy of Sciences, cod. H. 1667, fol. 195r (after Machavariani)

Among Armenian manuscripts as well we find at certain periods and in certain regions some very faithful copies of Constantinopolitan models, such as a Gospel book in San Lazzaro in Venice from about the tenth to eleventh century.[75] Its stately size, employed in Byzantium only for Lectionaries, and its full-page feast pictures, like that of the Metamorphosis (fig. 31),[76] indeed suggest that a Byzantine Lectionary served as its model. A nearly contemporary Byzantine parallel in an Athos codex in Iviron (fig. 32) shows essentially the same apostle types, though in mirror reversal: Peter kneeling and pointing at Christ, John falling to the ground, and James turning around to protect himself from the glaring light.[77] These are the types described by Nikolaos Mesarites in his *ekphrasis* of the Apostles' Church of Constantinople,[78] thus proving the Constantinopolitan origin of this particular iconography. But, as with the Georgian manuscripts, only with the more complete publication of the Armenian material—particularly the rich holdings of the museum at Erivan and the library of the Armenian Patriarchate of Jerusalem—will the extent of the influence of Byzantine book illumination become clear.

Byzantine influence penetrated even the world of the Christian Arabs, but since they were spread over many countries of the Near East, each with a very different cultural heritage, it was only to be expected that Byzantine models, while maintaining their iconography and compositional layout, would be cast into various local styles, like the Coptic, the Syrian, and, at a later period, even the Persian. There is at Sinai a copy of the *Scala Paradisi* of John Climacus, written in A.D. 1612 at Hama in Syria, which contains among its frontispieces the well-known composition of the Heavenly Ladder with the monks eagerly climbing, though many, stumbling, are snatched by devils and thrown into the gaping mouth of Hades (fig. 33).[79] Its source was surely a Byzantine miniature of the eleventh or twelfth century, more or less identical with a Sinai icon of that

75. M. Janashian, *Armenian Miniature Paintings of the Monastic Library at San Lazzaro* (Venice, 1966), pp. 23ff. and pls. 12–33.

76. Ibid., p. 26 and pl. 23. K. Weitzmann, *Die Armenische Buchmalerei des 10. und beginnenden 11. Jahrhunderts* (Bamberg, 1933), pp. 19ff. and pl. 13, fig. 47 (reprinted Amsterdam, 1970).

77. A. Xyngopoulos, *Evangiles avec miniatures du monastère d'Iviron au Mont Athos* (Athens, 1932), pp. 6ff. and pls. 1–2.

78. Weitzmann, "The Narrative and Liturgical Gospel Illustrations," *Studies*, pp. 260–61 and fig. 249. Idem, "A Metamorphosis Icon or Miniature on Mt. Sinai," *Starinar* 20 (1969), p. 416 and fig. 3.

79. S. Shenouda, "Sullan al-Fada il," *Majallat Kulliyat al'Adab* (Alexandria, U.A.R., 1969), pp. 163ff., pl. 1. Weitzmann, *Illustrated Manuscripts at St. Catherine's Monastery* (see note 8 above), pp. 31ff. and fig. 46.

Fig. 31. Metamorphosis. Venice, San Lazzaro, cod. 1400, fol. 4v

period (fig. 34).[80] In this case half a millenium separates the Byzantine model from its copy in Persian style in an Arabic manuscript.

Byzantine influence in the Arab world was not confined to the Christian Arabs, but penetrated also the Muslim culture, especially in the twelfth and thirteenth centuries. There is in the Topkapy Sarayi at Istanbul a luxuriously illustrated herbal of Dioscurides from the year A.D. 1229, with an author portrait (fig. 35)[81] which—and this is of particular importance—did not copy a classical portrait of Dioscurides like that in the famous sixth-century Juliana Anicia codex

80. K. Weitzmann, M. Chatzidakis, K. Miatev, S. Radojčić, *Frühe Ikonen* (Vienna and Munich, 1965), pp. XIII, LXXX, and pl. on p. 19.

81. R. Ettinghausen, *Arab Painting* (Lausanne, 1962), p. 67 and color plate, p. 69.

Fig. 32. Metamorphosis. Mount Athos, Iviron, cod. 1, fol. 303v

in Vienna,[82] but rather a classicizing evangelist of the Macedonian Renaissance, such as Matthew in a tenth-century Gospel book in Paris (fig. 36).[83] In composition as well as in minute details of drapery, the copyist followed his Byzantine model very closely indeed, adding merely a stately turban.

In all the Near Eastern cultures just discussed, Coptic, Syrian, Georgian,

82. Buberl, *Die Byzantinischen Handschriften*, vol. 1, pp. 24ff. and pls. 3–4. H. Gerstinger, *Dioscurides, Codex Vindobonensis med. gr. 1* (Graz, 1970), pp. 30ff. and plates fols. 4v and 5v.

83. Omont, *Miniatures*, p. 45 and pl. 81, fig. 1. Friend, "Evangelists" part 1, p. 130 and figs. 99–102. Weitzmann, *Byzantinische Buchmalerei*, p. 11 and pl. 11 fig. 57; pl. 12, fig. 60.

Fig. 33. Heavenly Ladder. Mount Sinai, cod. arab. 343, fol. 13v

41

Fig. 34. Heavenly Ladder. Mount Sinai. Icon

Fig. 35. Dioscurides. Istanbul, Topkapy Sarayi, cod. Ahmed. III 2127, fol. 1v

Armenian, and Arabic, Middle Byzantine influence was introduced into a native art with its own tradition, resulting in a mixture of varying degrees. In the Slavic countries one encounters quite a different situation. Here representational art started practically from scratch, copying Byzantine models as faithfully as possible on a vast scale, and this explains why Constantinopolitan influence is nowhere as strong and lasting as in the Balkan countries and Russia. Nowhere else, with the possible exception of a few instances in Georgia, were extensive Greek miniature cycles copied so frequently and in their entirety. There is, for instance, a Bulgarian Gospel Book from the year 1356 in London, British Museum cod. add. 39627,[84]

84. B. D. Filov, *Les Miniatures de l'Evangile du Roi Jean Alexandre à Londres* (Sofia, 1934). There exist three other Slavonic copies: see S. Der Nersessian, "Two Slavonic Parallels of the Greek Tetraevangelia: Paris 74," *Art Bulletin* 9 (1926–1927), pp. 223ff.

Fig. 36. Matthew. Paris, Bibliothèque Nationale, cod. Coislin 195, fol. 9v

that copies picture by picture the three to four hundred scenes of an eleventh-century Greek Gospel book in Paris, Bibl. Nat. cod. gr. 74.[85] Furthermore, there is a Psalter in the Public Library in Leningrad, written in Kiev in 1397 (fig. 37)[86] that copies with the same fidelity a Greek marginal Psalter of a branch surviving today only in a fragmentary copy from the eleventh to twelfth century in the Walters Art Gallery in Baltimore.[87] Hence this Russian Psalter becomes a

85. Omont, *Evangiles avec peintures* (see note 26 above).

86. *Licevaja psaltir 1397 goda prinadležaščaja Imperatorskomu Obščestvu ljubitelej drevnej pis'mennosti* (Saint Petersburg, 1890; lithographic facsimile). A. N. Svirin, *Iskusstvo Knigi Drevnei Rusi XI–XVIIb.b* (Moscow, 1964), p. 91f. and figs. on pp. 218–22.

87. D. E. Miner, "The 'Monastic' Psalter of the Walters Art Gallery," *Late Classical and Mediaeval Studies in Honor of Albert Mathias Friend, Jr.*, ed. K. Weitzmann (Princeton, 1955), pp. 232ff.

Fig. 37. Marginal Psalter. Leningrad, Public Library,
cod. 1252.F.VI (after Svirin)

document of primary importance for the history of Byzantine book illumination
as well, filling many lacunae in this particular cycle.

Of even greater importance are those Greek texts with pictures that survive
only in Slavic copies, such as the eleventh-century World Chronicle of Constantine Manasses, of which a Bulgarian copy from the fourteenth century is preserved
in the Vatican Library.[88] There can be no doubt that scenes such as those of the
pillaging Russians and the attack of the Byzantine emperor John Tzimisces on a
fortress in 972 (fig. 38) copy Byzantine models quite faithfully.[89] Moreover, there
exists a Russian translation of the Greek ninth-century World Chronicle of Georgios Hamartolos from the end of the thirteenth century in the Lenin Library in

88. B. Filov, *Miniatures de la Chronique de Manassès à la Bibliothèque du Vatican* (cod.
slav. 2) (Sofia, 1927). I. Dujčev, *The Miniatures of the Chronicle Manasse* (Sofia, 1963).
89. Filov, pls. 36 and 44. Dujčev, pl. miniature 64.

Fig. 38. Chronicle of Manasses. Rome, Vatican Library,
cod. slav. 2, fol. 178v (after Filov)

Moscow, just as richly illustrated but not yet completely published.[90] In view
of the fact that there exists today only a single illustrated chronicle in the Greek
language, a late-thirteenth-century copy of the eleventh-century original of John
Scylitzes in the National Library of Madrid, cod. 5-3, n. 2,[91] the Slavic copies of
the Manasses and the Georgios Hamartolos manuscripts provide evidence that
the Scylitzes is not an isolated example of Byzantine chronicle illustration. Apparently we are dealing here with a whole category of illustrated texts, and the suggestion that all major chronicles once had extensive miniature cycles seems not

90. N. P. Likhachev, *Materialy dlia Istorii Russkogo Ikonopisaniia*, vol 2 (St. Petersburg, 1906), pl. 261, figs. 718–19; and pl. 279. Svirin, *Iskusstvo*, p. 72f. and figs. on pp.
190–92.

91. S. P. Estopañan, *Skyllitzes Matritensis* (Barcelona and Madrid, 1965). A.
Boshkov, *Miniatjuri ot Madridskija R'kopis na Joan Skilitza* (Sofia, 1972).

inconceivable.[92] Thus the Slavic manuscripts fill a major gap in the history of Byzantine book illumination.

Most complex is the impact of Byzantine book illumination on the Latin West. Here Byzantine art was neither imposed upon a weaker partner, as it was in Coptic Egypt, or in Syria in the Middle Ages, nor did it form the foundation for a new start, as in the Slavic countries. After the downfall of the Roman empire, Latin art swung repeatedly between the two extremes of abstract and ornamental northern and anthropocentric southern forms. An intensification of Mediterranean influence, reviving the classical forms of Roman, Early Christian, and Early Byzantine art, began in the Carolingian period and from then on wave after wave of Byzantine influence swept over the European continent for about half a millennium, ending only in the Gothic period.[93] Each century and each country interpreted Byzantine art in its own way, but this is not the place to follow this process in detail; we shall confine ourselves to a few remarks about Carolingian book illumination and Biblical illustrations in particular.

Koehler, in his basic study on the manuscripts of Tours, fully realized that the frontispiece to the book of Genesis in the Grandval Bible in London (fig. 39), with its narrative scenes spanning the events from Adam's creation to his expulsion from Paradise, harks back to an archetype closely related to the Cotton Genesis (figs. 10, 11, and 18).[94] But while he considered the Genesis picture and three other full-page miniatures from this Touronian Bible faithful copies of an illustrated Bible made for Pope Leo the Great in the middle of the fifth century, it has recently been argued convincingly by Herbert Kessler that full Bibles with collective pictures heading individual books were a later invention.[95] All the extensive Early Christian cycles we have discussed illustrate only single books or sections

92. K. Weitzmann, "Illustrations for the Chronicles of Sozomenos, Theodoret and Malalas," *Byzantion* 16 (1944), pp. 87ff.

93. For the impact of Byzantine art, including book illumination, in the Latin West, see among others, W. Koehler, "Byzantine Art in the West," *Dumbarton Oaks Papers* 1 (1941), pp. 61ff.; K. Weitzmann, "Various Aspects of Byzantine Influence on the Latin Countries from the Sixth to the Twelfth Century," *Dumbarton Oaks Papers* 20 (1966), pp. 1ff.; E. Kitzinger, "The Byzantine Contribution to Western Art of the Twelfth and Thirteenth Centuries," *Dumbarton Oaks Papers* 20 (1966), pp. 25ff.; O. Demus, *Byzantine Art and the West* (New York, 1970); K. Weitzmann, "Byzantium and the West around the Year 1200," in the publication of the exhibition at the Metropolitan Museum, *The Year 1200*, vol. 3 (in press).

94. W. Koehler, *Die karolingischen Miniaturen*, vol. 1: *Die Schule von Tours*, part 2 (Berlin, 1933; reprinted 1963), pp. 118ff. and figs. 6–7.

95. H. L. Kessler, "The Sources and the Construction of the Genesis, Exodus, Majestas, and Apocalypse Frontispiece illustrations in the Ninth-Century Touronian Bibles" (Ph.D. diss., Department of Art and Archaeology, Princeton University, 1965). Idem, *The Illustrated Bibles from Tours* (in press).

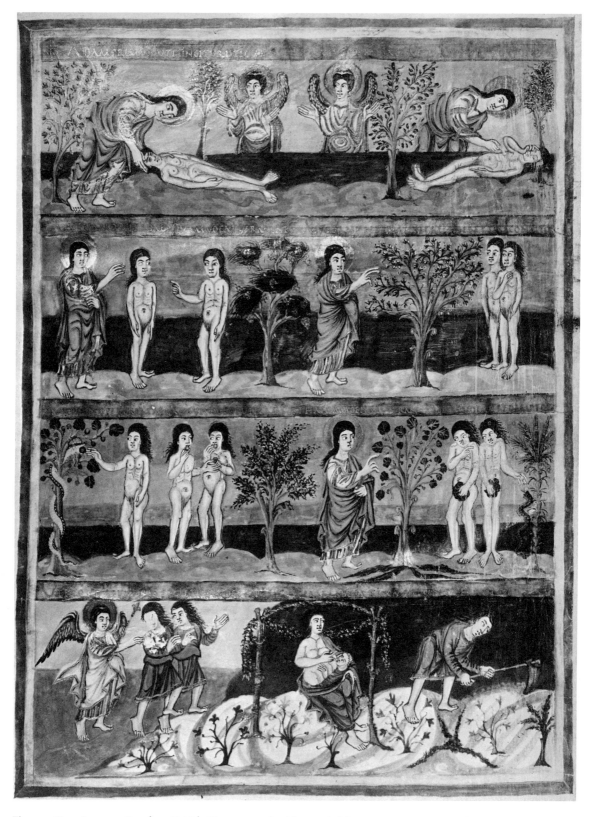

Fig. 39. Genesis scenes. London, British Museum, cod. add. 10546, fol. 5v

48

Fig. 40. Exodus scenes. Rome, San Paolo fuori le mura, fol. 20v

Fig. 41. Finding of the Child Moses. Rome, Vatican Library,
cod. gr. 747, fol. 72v

of the Old Testament; the reason for this is simply the practical impossibility
of decorating a full Bible on the scale in which the Cotton and the Vienna
Genesis were illustrated. One can only reconcile narrative illustration with the
textual bulk of the full Bible when cycles are epitomized on single huge pages
and distributed over several registers, and this apparently did not take place before
the Carolingian period.

Soon the number of sumptuous full-page miniatures grew, with the Bible in
San Paolo fuori le mura in Rome from about A.D. 870, made for Charles the Bald,
possessing no fewer than twenty-three.[96] At that time new sources had become

96. J. Gaehde, "The Painters of the Carolingian Bible Manuscript of San Paolo
fuori le mura in Rome" (Ph.D. diss., Institute of Fine Arts, New York, 1963). Idem,
"The Bible of San Paolo fuori le mura in Rome; its date and its relation to Charles the
Bald," *Gesta* 5 (1966), pp. 9ff. Idem, "The Touronian Sources of the Bible of San Paolo
fuori le Mura in Rome," *Frühmittelalterliche Studien: Jahrbuch des Instituts für Frühmittel-
alterforschung der Universität Münster* 5 (1971), pp. 350ff. Professor Gaehde is preparing a
facsimile edition of the San Paolo Bible.

available, as can clearly be demonstrated in the second Exodus picture, whose epitomized cycle begins with the Finding of Moses in the Nile (fig. 40).[97] The main figures in the center of the upper strip, where Pharaoh's daughter, in the presence of Miriam, orders a servant girl to descend into the water and fetch the little ark, agree iconographically so well with the corresponding figures in a miniature of an eleventh-century Octateuch in the Vatican (fig. 41) that there can be little doubt that both hark back to the same archetype, which can only have been a Greek Octateuch.

The importance of this comparison is twofold. First, it shows that the Carolingian artist, while choosing only a few episodes from the Book of Exodus for his frontispiece miniature, whereas the Octateuch has many more, nevertheless depicts the episode with the finding of Moses in much greater detail; in this respect the Carolingian miniature reflects the archetype better than the later Greek Octateuch. From this we learn that the Octateuchs, rich as they are, must in the course of repeated copying have been considerably reduced in the number of their scenes. The second point of importance is that the availability of a Greek Octateuch in the time of Charles the Bald must be viewed in the light of the intensified Byzantine influence after the end of Iconoclasm, when Byzantine art began to flourish anew and to exert a powerful influence upon late Carolingian art.[98] This was the first of several Byzantine waves that broke on European shores over half a millennium.

The Sixth Circle: Jewish Origins of Old Testament Illustration

It is not by chance that so much of our demonstration has centered on the extensive narrative cycles of the Bible, because it was here that Byzantine book illumination excelled. It has been pointed out that the earliest cycles are the richest, and this leads into the sixth circle, in which we will discuss the problem of the origin of the Old Testament cycles. Surely they did not spring like Athena from the head of Zeus, and the earliest extant cycles, such as those of the Vienna and Cotton Genesis, presuppose a long established tradition.

New light was cast on this problem in 1932 when an excavation by Yale University laid bare the frescoes with biblical scenes in the synagogue of Dura-Europos on the Euphrates, which must date before A.D. 256, when the Persians totally destroyed that city. The walls, of which about two-thirds still stand, now

97. Gaehde, "The Painters," pp. 493ff.

98. For the problem of the renewed Byzantine influence in the late Carolingian period, see K. Weitzmann, "The Origin of the Threnos," *De Artibus Opuscula XL: Essays in Honor of E. Panofsky* (New York, 1961), p. 482–83; idem, "Various Aspects," pp. 13–14 (see note 93 above).

in the Museum of Damascus, are decorated with three tiers of long friezes.[99] Their scenes were taken from the Books of Genesis, Exodus, Kings, Ezekiel, and Esther, and some of them narrate episodes in successive phases over long strips, deploying a method typical of book illumination. Thus we believe that the frescoes are actually derived from illustrated manuscripts, which presupposes, of course, that this type of painting was exercised in the communities of hellenized Jews. While some scholars are still unwilling to accept this premise, others, myself among them, do so for various reasons.[100] First of all, in analyzing such a frieze as that with the Infancy of Moses (fig. 42),[101] we see that there prevails the same principle of adaptation of miniatures as in the copy of the Cotton Genesis miniatures by the San Marco mosaicists (figs. 18 and 19), that is, extreme condensation because of restricted space. Pharaoh ordering the killing of the Jewish offspring and the exposure of the infant Moses in the Nile would be two separate, successive scenes in a manuscript, and this condensation, or rather conflation, goes even further in the left half of the frescoe, where there are contracted in simultaneous action three phases that in the manuscript model must have been separate: the recovery of the ark, the handing of Moses to Miriam, and her handing him to Jochebed. To judge from this and other frescoes like the Crossing of the Red Sea[102] or the Vision of Ezekiel,[103] the underlying miniature cycles must have been very vast, since the frescoes are apparently only epitomes. In this way Dura gives us insight into an otherwise lost branch of art, which must have produced narrative cycles on a grand scale.

A second aspect of this problem, and the one that interests us most, is whether these Jewish Old Testament cycles were consulted and copied by the Christians when they began to illustrate their manuscripts. This question has been answered negatively by some scholars[104] and positively by others. To the latter persuasion belongs Du Mesnil du Buisson who, in the first serious treatment of the frescoes, introduced the Exodus miniature of the San Paolo Bible (fig. 40) as proof of such

99. For the most authoritative statement on the Dura frescoes, the bibliography for which has mushroomed, see Carl H. Kraeling, *The Synagogue: The Excavations at Dura-Europos. Final Report*, vol. 8, part 1 (New Haven, 1956).

100. For a collection of articles discussing this vital issue, see, *No Graven Images: Studies in Art and the Hebrew Bible*, J. Gutman ed. (New York, 1970).

101. Kraeling, *The Synagogue*, pp. 169ff. and pls. 67–68. Weitzmann, "Illustration of the Septuagint," *Studies*, pp. 71ff. and figs. 53–54.

102. Kraeling, *The Synagogue*, pp. 74ff. and pls. 52–53.

103. Ibid., pp. 178ff. and pls. 69–71. K. Weitzmann, "Narration in Ancient Art," *American Journal of Archaeology* 61 (1957), p. 89 and pl. 36, fig. 14.

104. For a negative answer, cf. C. R. Morey, *Early Christian Art*, 2d ed. (Princeton, 1953), pp. 65, 77.

a connection, pointing specifically to the figure of Jochebed in the action of setting afloat the ark.[105]

As stated before, this Carolingian miniature stands in the tradition of the Greek Octateuchs, in which there is further proof of the connection between the Dura frescoes and the Christian tradition. In the Vatican manuscript gr. 747—and in this copy only—we find the extremely rare scene of Pharaoh ordering the two midwives Shiphrah and Puah to kill the Jewish menchildren (fig. 43)[106] in a composition that agrees sufficiently in its essential points with the Dura fresco to justify the assumption of a common archetype. Nor is this the only example of an iconographic relationship between the Dura frescoes and Greek miniatures.[107]

Though Dura in our opinion would be sufficient proof of the existence of Jewish book illumination and its influence upon the Christian, it is not the only proof available. Once the problem with all its implications was realized, a careful investigation of Septuagint illustrations revealed that many other scenes as well, not included among the Dura frescoes, contain elements that cannot be explained by the Bible text but only by Jewish legends. The obvious conclusion, then, is that such scenes originated in Jewish legendary of apocryphal texts that had gained a certain popularity and were available to the first Christians who illustrated the Old Testament. Quite a number of such scenes have been identified within the Octateuchs, a rich hunting ground for that purpose. In the scene of Eve's temptation, for instance, the serpent is depicted mounting a camel, an obscure feature that can be explained by a passage in the so-called *Pirke* of Rabbi Eliezer;[108] similarly, the scene of Cain slaying Abel by pelting him with stones is a feature best explained by the Haggadah.[109]

To these may be added another example. Where the Septuagint merely says, "Sarah saw the son of Hagar mocking," a miniature in one of the Vatican Octateuchs (fig. 44) depicts the aftermath of an actual fight, in which Ishmael has apparently hit Isaac so hard that his nose is bleeding. Such a feature might be explained by a phrase in Flavius Josephus' *Antiquitates Judaicae* (I.XII.3), where Sarah expresses fear that Ishmael "might do some injury to Isaac."[110]

Nor are the Octateuchs the only Greek manuscripts that contain elements of

105. Comte Du Mesnil du Buisson, *Les Peintures de la Synagogue de Doura-Europos 245–256 après J.-C.* (Rome, 1939), p. 124 and pl. 1a.

106. Weitzmann, "Octateuch" (see note 57 above), pp. 185 and fig. 5. Idem, "Illustration of the Septuagint," *Studies*, p. 72 and fig. 55.

107. In four lectures at a symposium at Dumbarton Oaks in 1945, these connections were discussed at some length and will be published in the Princeton series *Studies in Manuscript Illumination*.

108. Weitzmann, "Illustration of the Septuagint," *Studies*, p. 74 and fig. 56.

109. Weitzmann, "Jewish Pictorial Sources," *Studies*, p. 83 and fig. 62.

110. H. St. J. Thackeray, *Josephus*, vol. 1, Loeb Classical Library (London, 1930), p. 107.

Fig. 42. Infancy of Moses. Damascus, Museum. Synagogue of Dura. Fresco

Fig. 43. Pharaoh's Order.
Rome, Vatican Library,
cod. gr. 747, fol. 72r

Fig. 44. Sarah with Ishmael and Isaac. Rome, Vatican Library, cod. gr. 746, fol. 80r

Jewish legends. Such elements abound in the Vienna Genesis,[111] and they occur as well in the Cotton Genesis[112] and in the Sacra Parallela in Paris.[113]

All this evidence indicates that Jewish book illumination must have spread widely and that we are only beginning to explore a new field of investigation in which not only pictorial but also textual evidence must be gathered from many sources, since we apparently are dealing with a variety of texts that the hellenized Jews must have enjoyed seeing adorned with extensive picture cycles.

The Seventh Circle: Invention of Narrative Illustration in Greco-Roman Art

The Jews can hardly be credited with having invented a method of such far-reaching consequences as pictorial narration. Such an invention would have to have occurred in the climate of a tradition that was accustomed to transforming

111. O. Pächt, "Ephraimillustration, Haggadah und Wiener Genesis," *Festschrift Karl M. Swoboda* (Vienna, 1959), pp. 213ff. Weitzmann, "Jewish Pictorial Sources," *Studies*, pp. 84ff. and fig. 64. Most recently, M. Levin, "Some Jewish Sources for the Vienna Genesis," *Art Bulletin* 54 (1972), pp. 241ff., and E. Revel, "Contribution des textes rabbiniques à l'étude de la Genèse de Vienna," *Byzantion* 42 (1972), pp. 115ff.

112. Weitzmann, "Jewish Pictorial Sources," *Studies*, pp. 88ff. and fig. 67. H. Kessler, "Hic Homo Formatur: The Genesis Frontispiece of the Carolingian Bibles," *Art Bulletin* 52 (1971), p. 155.

113. Weitzmann, "Jewish Pictorial Sources," *Studies*, pp. 85ff. and figs. 65–66.

rich and colorful literary content into eloquent pictorial language. It could only have happened within the Greco-Roman culture. The Jews and the Christians alike had started out with a hostile attitude toward representational art, and began to accept it only when they adapted the Greco-Roman way of life with all its urban amenities, including the love of art in all its complexity and richness.

That the Greeks had illustrated their papyrus rolls there can be no doubt, although, because of the perishability of the material, little has survived.[114] Among the few fragments is an Oxyrhynchus papyrus of the third century A.D., which contains a Heracles poem and, in typical papyrus fashion, a few washed pen drawings depicting Heracles' lion fight strewn through the text where they are most appropriate (fig. 45).[115] This is not the place to demonstrate the extent of classical book illumination. Let it suffice to say that the principal texts to be adorned with illustrations were, in our opinion, the Homeric poems, as well as other epics, and dramas, foremost those of Euripides. Novels of different kinds as well, bucolic poetry, fables, biographical texts, and still others were apparently illustrated prolifically. As in the case of the Jewish texts, this raises once more the question of whether the Christians had knowledge of classical book illumination, and whether they made use of it.

In the repeatedly cited Vatican Octateuch cod. gr. 747, there is a scene of Samson Fighting the Lion, where he employs the same kind of firm grip as Heracles, clamping the lion's head under his armpit (fig. 46).[116] There can be little doubt that the first Biblical illustrator, at a time when classical mythology was still widely understood, was inspired by a representation of Heracles' lion fight and copied it very closely, the clothing of the Biblical hero being the only major alteration.

We are not dealing with an isolated case here, and it can be demonstrated that the use of classical models was widespread in the early phases of Christian art. It almost appears that the Bible illustrators, when suddenly faced for the first time with the enormous task of illustrating the individual books of the Old Testament on a vast scale, actually combed the illustrations of ancient texts, not merely to find fitting figure types, but for whole classical compositions of similar meaning,

114. For a methodological study that discusses the origin of ancient book illumination and its method of illustration see Weitzmann, *Roll and Codex*, 2d ed., and for a historical study dealing with the variety of ancient texts illustrated, see Weitzmann, *Ancient Book Illumination* (Cambridge, Mass., 1959).

115. K. Weitzmann, in *The Oxyrhynchus Papyri*, pt. 22, no. 2331 (London, 1954), pp. 85ff. and pl. 11. Idem, *Ancient Book Illumination*, p. 53 and pl. 26, fig. 59. Idem, *Roll and Codex*, 2d ed., p. 239 and pl. 15, fig. 40a.

116. K. Weitzmann, "The Survival of Mythological Representations in Early Christian and Byzantine Art and their Impact on Christian Iconography," *Dumbarton Oaks Papers* 14 (1960), p. 58 and figs. 25–26.

Fig. 45. Heracles Poem. London, Egypt Exploration Society, pap. gr. Oxy. 2331

Fig. 46. Samson Fighting the Lion. Rome, Vatican Library, cod. gr. 747, fol. 248v

which they still understood and quite often needed to change only slightly to adjust them to the Biblical text. A striking example is presented by the Creation of Adam. In the recension centering around the Cotton Genesis, to which belong, as we have mentioned before, the San Marco mosaics (fig. 19) and the Touronian Bibles (fig. 39), the Creation of Adam is depicted in three distinct phases (figs. 47–49): the Creator, in human form, shaping Adam like a sculptor his clay; then infusing the spark of life by touching Adam's head from behind; and finally introducing the soul, in the form of a butterfly, into Adam's mouth.[117] These three stages of the Creation correspond exactly to those of the creation of man by Prometheus, and we likewise find on Roman sarcophagi the Shaping, Enlivenment, and Animation (figs. 50–52). Surely the Biblical illustrator did not study Roman sarcophagi, but rather had a model in which the three phases were united in their proper sequence; in our opinion, this could only have been a manuscript, most likely a Greek mythological handbook, comparable to the Bulfinch of our time. We have evidence of an illustrated mythological handbook, the *Bibliotheke* attributed to Apollodorus;[118] this could not have been the model for the Creation scenes, but Apollodorus' was not the only such mythological handbook in classical antiquity.

There exist Biblical illustrations that adapted and readjusted compositional schemes from the *Iliad* and the poems of the Trojan cycle, others that made use of compositions from illustrated dramas, and still others.[119] So far we have only begun to explore this wide-open area.

Realizing that the farther the distance from the stone's throw, the less distinct the ripple's profile, in our seventh circle we have reached a realm where the basic materials, that is, the illustrated rolls, are very scarce and where we must rely to a greater extent on inference. Even so, we believe that this seventh circle is still distinctly recognizable. But does it reach the shore? Have the ripples on the surface of the water spent their energy? The peculiar method of pictorial narration wherein an episode like that of the Creation scenes is illustrated in many phases in a rapid succession so that the story may be read from the pictures without resorting to the text, is the invention of the Hellenistic period. Most likely it was conceived at Alexandria, the center of learning in the ancient world, where

117. Weitzmann, *Roll and Codex*, 2d ed., pp. 176ff., 257, and pl. 51. Idem, "Illustration of the Septuagint," *Studies*, pp. 69ff. and figs. 47–52.

118. K. Weitzmann, *Greek Mythology in Byzantine Art* (Princeton, 1951), pp. 78ff. and passim.

119. Weitzmann, *Roll and Codex*, 2d ed., pp. 174ff. and pl. 50, figs. 173–176. Idem, "Survival," pp. 58ff. and figs. 27–33.

Fig. 47. Shaping of Adam.
Venice, San Marco. Mosaic

Fig. 48. Enlivenment of Adam. London, British Museum,
cod. add. 10546, fol. 5v

Fig. 49. Animation of Adam. Venice, San Marco. Mosaic

Fig. 50. Shaping of Man.
Rome, Vatican. Sarcophagus

Fig. 51. Enlivenment of Man. Naples, Museo Nazionale. Sarcophagus

Fig. 52. Animation of Man. Rome, Museo Capitolino. Sarcophagus

books were first mass-produced—a precondition, along with the popularity of texts, for their illustration. Could there be an eighth circle, leading further back into the ancient Orient, perhaps to Egypt, where not only the Book of the Dead but other texts as well were richly illustrated? Here I shall stop and pass on the torch of investigation to the scholar versed in the ancient Orient.[120]

It must by now have become clear that most of the work done thus far— and it is only right that this should be so—has concentrated on the inner circles, and that the wider the circles, the greater the gaps to be bridged. As for the outer circles, hardly more has been formulated than programs of future research, whose aim it must be to achieve a better understanding of the continuity of our Western civilization, from the Greco-Roman to the Jewish and finally to the Christian.

120. This problem was discussed at a symposium of the fifty-seventh meeting of the Archaeological Institute of America in Chicago conducted by the late Carl Kraeling. See especially the papers on Egypt by Helene Cantor, Babylonia by Ann Perkins, and Anatolia, Syria, and Assyria by Hans Güterbock, *American Journal of Archaeology* 61 (1957), pp. 43ff.

William C. Loerke

The Monumental Miniature

Byzantine art concerns itself chiefly with Biblical subjects whose Biblical texts are repeatedly read in the liturgy. Representations of these subjects fall into a limited number of types, which are repeated with variations time and again in different media. That examples of the same type of a given scene can be found in different media opens the question of the origin of the type and the medium in which it first occurred. In this paper I shall deal with miniatures whose composition betrays a derivation from monumental wall painting.

The notion that we can expect to find and do find in Byzantine miniatures a record of lost Byzantine wall painting was an article of faith for Kondakov, Dobbert, and Haseloff in the last quarter of the last century,[1] and for Muñoz, Dalton, Wulff, Diehl, and Gerstinger in the first half of this century.[2] It was also an article of faith for A. M. Friend, Jr. In seminars in Princeton and in a symposium held in 1948 at Dumbarton Oaks, "The Church of the Holy Apostles, Constantinople," he mounted a broad, sustained, and ingenious assault on this problem. In his hands, an iconographic and stylistic problem became an art-historical crusade

1. N. Kondakov, *Histoire de l'Art Byzantin*, vol. 1 (Paris, 1886), pp. 32 and 116. E. Dobbert, "Das Abendmahl Christi in der bildenden Kunst," *Repertorium für Kunstwissenschaft* 14 (Berlin, 1891), p. 455. A. Haseloff, *Codex purpureus Rossanensis* (Berlin and Leipzig, 1898), pp. 48, 103, 122. H. Graeven, review of Haseloff, in *Göttingische Gelehrte Anzeigen* (1900), pp. 423–29.

2. A. Muñoz, *Il codice purpureo di Rossano* (Rome, 1907), pp. 14, 26. O. M. Dalton, *Byzantine Art and Archaeology* (Oxford, 1911), p. 454. O. Wulff, *Altchristliche und Byzantinische Kunst* (Berlin, 1913), p. 302. C. Diehl, *Manuel d'art byzantin*, vol. 1 (Paris, 1925), pp. 255–58. H. Gerstinger, *Die Griechische Buchmalerei* (Vienna, 1926), p. 19a.

William C. Loerke

to recapture the lost ecclesiastical walls of Jerusalem and Constantinople with their presumed mosaics intact.

Articles of faith do not necessarily attract believers through repetition. The writer of the Epistle to the Hebrews defined faith as "the evidence of things not seen," a definition painfully appropriate to assertions about monumental sources for miniature painting. And yet the problem continues a shadowy life in the passing reference and untested hypothesis. To suggest that early manuscript illumination contains a record of early wall paintings is clearly not news. But to reexamine the miniatures remains worthwhile. Let us confront the evidence to see whether those traits that led so many Byzantine scholars to assume the presence of monumental originals cannot now prove the same.

As in so many cases, the discussion cannot continue in the old frames of reference. The chief reason that this is so can be found in the achievements of the scholar in whose honor these papers are presented. Kurt Weitzmann has fundamentally recast the terms in which we study the relation between text and image.[3] He has opened up new paths between miniature and icon painting,[4] and refined the criteria by which we can distinguish between narrative and liturgical Gospel illustrations.[5] In short, he has laid fresh foundations for those who address themselves to this topic. I hope he will accept my foray into this thorny problem as a tribute of a grateful student and an old friend.

The lost monumental paintings of Early Christian art have been the apocrypha of Byzantine art historiography for a century. How can they enter the canon? Obviously only with the aid and consent of their progeny. Among their presumed progeny are works in a variety of media, chief among which is manuscript illumination. The miniatures that most impressed the scholars mentioned above as being copies of monumental painting are the following: the final full-page compositions of the Rabula Gospels, like the Ascension and Pentecost; all the miniatures of the Rossano Gospels; and selected miniatures of the Vatican Cosmas Indicopleustes. In 1879, Bayet remarked of the standing figures on folio 76 of the Vatican Cosmas (fig. 1): "I am not far from believing that this miniature has been copied from a mosaic." Still, he was far enough from believing it to place

3. K. Weitzmann, *Illustrations in Roll and Codex: A Study of the Origin and Method of Text Illustration*, 2d ed. (Princeton, 1970).

4. Idem, "Byzantine Miniature and Icon Painting in the Eleventh Century," *Proceedings of the XIIIth International Congress of Byzantine Studies* (London, 1967), pp. 207–24 (reprinted in *Studies in Classical and Byzantine Manuscript Illumination*, ed. H. L. Kessler [Chicago, 1971], pp. 271–313).

5. Idem, "The Narrative and Liturgical Gospel Illustrations," *New Testament Manuscript Studies*, ed. M. Parvis and A. Wikgren (Chicago, 1950) (reprinted in *Studies* [see note 4 above], pp. 247–70).

that remark in a footnote, as if uttered *sotto voce*.[6] Nor did he confront the problem presented by a wall painting that would show the Baptist directly on axis and Christ to one side.[7] Bayet, of course, believed that miniaturists of the eighth and ninth centuries copied images from older illuminated manuscripts. But he also believed that "he whose works they copied had not created those images. Closer to the third and fourth centuries he knew the monumental originals. He was inspired by paintings that decorated churches and primitive crypts."[8]

Kondakov appreciated "the antique grandeur, the breadth, solidity, and placidity of these figures." He felt that "the iconographic tradition has imposed on all the compositions of the Cosmas manuscript the character of monumental painting," and that among the models for these miniatures were "the oldest mosaics of Saloniki," like the figure of Saint Paul in Saint Sophia (fig. 2), which he then took to be pre-Iconoclastic in date.[9] These observations rely heavily on the recognition of a monumental scale, character, and style in individual figures of certain miniatures. This monumental quality, however, could reflect the general impact of monumental painting upon the work of the miniaturist.

In a series of masterly studies developing the concept of the Macedonian Renaissance, Weitzmann provided another, less monumental explanation for the "antique grandeur" that Kondakov rightly perceived.[10] He showed how the use of classical models proliferated in the period after the Iconoclastic controversy, in a setting that Constantine Porphyrogenitus himself described as a "rebirth" and "renewal." Antique grandeur and monumental scale in individual figures in a miniature no longer suffice to prove descent from a monumental prototype.

At the turn of the century, Haseloff and Ainalov brought criteria more probing than those of Bayet and Kondakov to bear upon the problem of identifying lost monumental paintings in miniature copies. These criteria they derived chiefly from a comparative study of the miniatures in the Rossano Gospels and

6. C. Bayet, *Recherches pour servir à l'histoire de la peinture* . . . (Paris, 1879), p. 71, note 1.

7. C. Stornajolo, *Le miniature della Topografia cristiana di Cosma Indicopleuste, Codice Vaticano Greco 699* (Milan, 1908), p. 42, note 6, called attention to this unusual aspect of the composition without offering an adequate explanation. For the setting of this miniature in Book Five of Cosmas' *Topography*, see H. Graeven, "Die Madonna zwischen Zacharias und Johannes," *Byzantinische Zeitschrift* 10 (1901), pp. 1–22, esp. 6f.

8. Bayet, *Recherches*, p. 21f.

9. Kondakov, *Histoire*, pp. 135, 139.

10. K. Weitzmann, "Der Pariser Psalter ms. grec 139 und die mittelbyzantinische Renaissance," *Jahrbuch für Kunstgeschichte* 7 (1929), pp. 178ff. Idem, "The Classical Heritage in the Art of Constantinople," *Studies*, pp. 126–50. Idem, "The Classical in Byzantine Art as a Mode of Individual Expression," *Byzantine Art: An European Art* (Athens, 1966), pp. 149–77 (reprinted in *Studies*, pp. 151–75). Idem, "The Character and Intellectual Origins of the Macedonian Renaissance," *Studies*, pp. 176–223.

Fig. 1. The Virgin, Christ, John the Baptist, Zachariah, Elizabeth. Rome, Vatican Library, cod. gr. 699 (Christian Topography of Cosmas Indicopleustes), fol. 76r

those of the Vienna Genesis.[11] From a stylistic analysis, Ainalov concluded that "there can be no doubt that various originals were copied in order to decorate the Vienna Genesis. Just as the Rossano Gospel book reproduces monumental compositions, so the Vienna Genesis reproduces the style of at least two manuscripts."[12] From a compositional analysis, he asserted that "the traditions of miniature painting are totally lacking in the Rossano manuscript. This is the first and foremost characteristic of the drawings of this Gospel. All the images bear the imprint of monumental style. The relief-like quality displayed in the disposition of figures in rows seems to indicate that the illuminations of this manuscript were

11. Haseloff, *Rossanensis*, pp. 121–23. D. Ainalov, *The Hellenistic Origins of Byzantine Art*, ed. C. Mango (New Brunswick, 1961), pp. 124ff.

12. Ainalov, *Origins*, p. 126.

Fig. 2. Paul. Salonika, Saint Sophia, Ascension dome. Mosaic
(detail)

direct copies from monumental friezes."[13] These seventy-year-old observations
still offer good guidance to those who wish to identify miniature copies of monumental originals. The lesson is: analyze the compositions as well as the individual
figures.

I shall begin another assault on this old and difficult problem by showing an undisputed case where a miniature is the copy of a wall mosaic—undisputed because
both miniature and mosaic survive. We owe this example to Hugo Buchthal,
who found two late-thirteenth-century miniatures that copied late-twelfth-
century mosaics in the side aisle of the Cathedral of Monreale.[14] The miniatures

13. Ibid., p. 108f.
14. H. Buchthal, "Some Sicilian Miniatures of the Thirteenth Century," *Miscellanea Pro Arte: Festschrift für Hermann Schnitzler* (Düsseldorf, 1965), pp. 185–90.

Fig. 3. Healing of the Paralytic. Stockholm, National Museum. Leaf from Gospel book

occupy the lower right corner of recto pages that have been cut from a Gospel book. One miniature, in the Uffizi, shows Christ healing Peter's mother-in-law; the other, in Stockholm, shows the Healing of the Paralytic (fig. 3).

It is instructive to observe changes wrought by the transfer of these compositions from the wall (fig. 4) to the book. Buchthal has pointed these out in detail and I wish to call attention only to two of them. The architectural background in the right half of the Stockholm miniature has expanded vertically in the space available in the right-hand margin of the page. The scene as a whole, however, was composed and reduced for the bottom margin, the proportions of which differ substantially from those of the wall mosaic. On the wall, the width of the assigned space is about three quarters of its height. The bottom margin of the page reverses these proportions. The broad proportions of this bottom margin allowed and perhaps induced the miniaturist to expand his composition laterally. These physical discrepancies between miniature copy and monumental original can be attributed to the conversion of the composition from one format to another.

Fig. 4. Healing of the Paralytic. Monreale, Cathedral. Mosaic

A stylistic discrepancy between miniature and mosaic is also apparent. While he has followed the composition as well as he could in the new format, the miniaturist has betrayed his own late-thirteenth-century Italian hand in the postures, proportions, and soft style of the figures. In addition, those figures that, in the mosaic, observe the observer in Byzantine fashion and call the miracle to his attention, have given up this function in the miniature. They immerse themselves fully in the narrative. The essentially narrative character of thirteenth-century manuscript illumination has overcome the public didactic character of twelfth-century Byzantine wall painting.

Suppose the monumental originals had been lost. Could we have surmised their existence from these miniatures? Quite possibly, if we had noticed the unusually tall proportions of the structure on the right, out of scale with the rest of the architectural background. This tall structure wrongly places major emphasis on minor attendants. If we correct this error by visualizing the entire architectural background in the same size and scale as the right-hand member, we might then suspect we were looking at a copy of a monumental original. In any case, it is clearly necessary to the identification of a miniature copy of a monumental original that some dislocation be preserved and identified in the miniature, as a record of the transfer from wall to book.

Three physical dislocations of precisely this sort, once identified, revealed that the full-page miniatures of the Trial of Christ before Pilate in the Rossano Gospels were copies of monumental originals,[15] as Haseloff and others had asserted.[16] The dislocations are all in the second miniature, folio 8v (fig. 5), and not in the first, folio 8r. They concern first the strange disposition of the crowds, with their heads against the semicircular blue line, their feet abandoning the ground line; second, the poor spacing of the two groups in the lower register; third, the poor communication between the two registers. These problems are all resolved by casting this composition into an apse (fig. 6). The additional lateral space provided by the curving wall would then offer sufficient room for the crowd to come down onto the ground line without overlapping the tribunal. Windows beneath the tribunal separate the two groups below into a balanced contrast between Christ and Barabbas, thus emphasizing the central point of the whole composition, that is, the choice between Christ and Barabbas. With the groups thus separated in the apse, Pilate's right hand actually points to Christ, as it should, rather than to the official at the extreme left, as it does in the miniature. Barabbas' jailer looks up to see what Pilate's decision will be. In the miniature, his gaze passes to the left of Pilate; in the apse, he looks directly at him. The semicircular blue line in this miniature records the front face of the conch of the apse. In the first Trial miniature, where no aberrations like these occur in the composition, the semicircular blue line is the record of a relieving arch crowning a flat wall. We may imagine the monumental originals of these miniatures in an architectural setting like the choir and apse of San Vitale.

One further lesson about monumental miniatures may be drawn from this example. The case for monumental originals for these two miniatures does not rest upon the style of individual figures, some of which are monumental in character while others are not. One could compare the officials wearing the chlamys in these scenes with figures in the Justinian mosaic in San Vitale of the sixth century, and with official statuary from Aphrodisias and Corinth of the first half of the fifth century to show how closely they parallel monumental examples. On the other hand, the closest parallels to the two officials flanking Christ in the second miniature can be found in the Vienna Genesis, in Potiphar and his associate (*pictura* 32), in a scene for which no one would suggest a monumental prototype.

15. W. Loerke, "The Trials of Christ in the Rossano Gospels," *Art Bulletin* 43 (1961), pp. 186ff.

16. Haseloff, *Rossanensis*, pp. 48f., 122f. Graeven, in *Göttingische Gelehrte Anzeigen*, p. 426. Ainalov, *Origins*, p. 109.

The Trial scenes in the Rossano Gospels are unique among the Gospel scenes of this manuscript in that they alone occupy full pages. The miniatures that precede them are presented in broad friezes set above Old Testament Prophets, holding scrolls on which their prophecies can be read. In most cases, these frieze-like compositions are the earliest examples of an iconography that became standard and widespread in later Byzantine art, both on the wall and in the book. The question is: how did this iconography become the norm?

The manuscript in Rossano cannot account for any of the later representations in miniatures, icons, frescoes, or mosaics modeled on the compositions of its own miniatures. It is far more likely that the miniatures of this manuscript are the oldest record of a public presentation of these compositions, sufficiently prominent to account for their proliferation in a variety of media in later Byzantine art. Ainalov doubtless assumed this when he asserted that all the Rossano miniatures derived from monumental originals. In 1900, Graeven had cited the presence of Old Testament Prophets below New Testament scenes as a reason for assuming a monumental source.[17] These miniatures of the Rossano Gospels with their prophetic commentary constitute a *Concordia veteris et novi testamenti.* Was this *Concordia* originally designed for the walls of a church?

The Rossano Gospels belong to that limited number of illuminated Gospel books that place all the miniatures at the front. Two points have been reiterated about this series as a whole: one, that it is liturgical in character, and two, that it derives from a monumental prototype. Since the first of these points is relevant to the second, I should like to begin by showing how these pages are liturgical compositions.

The selection and sequence of scenes in this cycle cannot be explained by the continuous text of any one Gospel; to account for this sequence, one must appeal to the standard sequence of readings of the Greek liturgy. From the *Raising of Lazarus,* folio 1r, to the Trial scenes of folio 8, we find that the sequence follows the readings from the Saturday before Palm Sunday through Good Friday.[18] The texts of these miniatures lie in three Gospels and it is only in the spoken liturgy, or in a service book prepared for liturgical use, that is, a Lectionary, that we encounter these texts in the order of these miniatures. The forty verses form twenty pairs, in nineteen of which David occurs, paired with a Prophet sixteen times and with himself three times. With the exception of folio 4, he occupies the first and third positions on the page. These pairs reflect the liturgical practice in which a Psalm verse, a *stichos,* normally preceded Old and New Testament lessons.[19]

17. Graeven, op. cit., p. 423.

18. F. Conybeare, *Rituale Armenorum* (Oxford, 1905), p. 520f. M. Tarchnischvili, *Le Grand Lectionnaire de l'Eglise de Jérusalem,* vol. 1 (Louvain, 1959), pp. 80–96.

19. Tarchnischvili, *Lectionnaire,* passim.

Fig. 5. Trial of Christ before Pilate. Rossano, Archepiscopal Treasury, Rossano Gospels, fol. 8v

Fig. 6. Model of apse based on fol. 8v, Rossano Gospels

William C. Loerke

Granted that the miniatures owe their selection and sequence to the liturgy, and that the Old Testament verses below owe their selection and pairing to the liturgy, what is the visual relationship between the miniatures and the texts? In the case of the *Parable of the Ten Virgins* (fig. 7), the two verses below the Wise Virgins apply to the Foolish, and vice versa. Under the Wise Virgins, we find Psalm 52:6, "They were ashamed for God despised them," and Hosea 7:13, "Woe to them for they started aside from me. . . ." Under the Foolish Virgins are two citations from Psalm 44: verses 15, "Virgins shall be brought to the king after her," and 14, "All her glory is that of the daughter of the king within." These verses apply to that part of the scene to which the psalmist or Prophet points. We are to view these pages as full-page compositions, whose chiastic order integrates visually the prophetic word of the Old Testament with the imaged deed or parable of the New.

The same principle of visual-verbal chiastic composition can be observed on folio 3r, where two events are depicted: the historical *Last Supper* at the left, as in Matthew 26:20–24, and the *Washing of the Feet* at the right, told only in John 13:3–30 (fig. 8). The pair of verses at the left, below the *Last Supper*, refers to the *Washing of the Feet*; the pair at the right, below the *Washing of the Feet*, refers to the *Last Supper*. The left pair consists of Psalm 22:2, "By the waters of rest, he nourishes me;" and Psalm 40:10, "The one eating my bread lifted up his heel against me," a verse quoted by Jesus, according to John 13:18, at the Washing of the Feet. The first verse of the right pair is Psalm 40:7–8, "He went forth and spoke in like manner. Against me did all my enemies whisper;" and the second is Zephaniah 1:7, "Fear ye before the face of the Lord . . . for . . . the Lord has prepared his sacrifice."[20]

The three Psalm verses on this page were used in services on Holy Thursday in fifth-century Jerusalem. Psalm 22:2 is prescribed in the canon as a *stichos* preceding four New Testament lessons, which included I Corinthians 11:23–32, the Communion; Matthew 26:20–24, the Last Supper; and John 13:3–30, the Washing of the Feet.[21] The verses from Psalm 40, aimed against Judas, prefaced a reading of Matthew 26:2–16, which ends with Judas' resolution to betray Christ.[22] Christ predicts this resolution and exposes it at the Last Supper in words that form the inscription over the miniature: "Verily I say unto you, one of you shall betray me" (Matt. 26:21). Judas' hand in the dish in the miniature identifies the betrayer, as stated two verses later: "He that dippeth his hand in the dish, the same shall betray me" (Matt. 26:23).

On this page, as in the liturgy, we pass verbally from Psalm 40 to Matthew 26, verse 21 in the inscription and visually to verse 23 in the miniature. The whole

20. For the numbering of the Psalms and verses, I am following the Septuagint edition of A. Rahlfs. For the Greek texts as transcribed from this folio, see Muñoz, *Codice purpureo*, p. 6.

21. Tarchnischvili, *Lectionnaire*, p. 91.

22. Ibid., p. 89.

page is surely a liturgical composition, recalling to the reader the divine service in which the life of Christ annually unfolded before him in carefully selected and integrated readings from Psalms, the Prophets, and the Gospels. Texts and images on this page form not only a *Concordia veteris et novi testamenti*, but record a particular *Concordia* created for the liturgy.

Why does this liturgical composition appear in a Gospel book? Was it copied from a lost Lectionary, a service book whose unique textual sequence (Matt. 26 to John 13) alone justifies these two scenes on one page? About this we can only speculate, since no Lectionary survives from the period before the tenth century. Was this composition on folio 3r devised originally for the walls of a basilica, as a public record of the liturgy celebrated therein? Either alternative is attractive to those of us who like to believe that the original context of a work of art is somehow integral with its character and composition. Either a page of a Lectionary or the interior wall of a basilica defines a birthplace inherently more fitting for a liturgical composition than a leaf of a Gospel book, however sumptuous.

Whatever the explanation, these miniatures have clearly been copied from something, whether another miniature or a monumental prototype. In the case of the *Washing of the Feet*, observe the direction in which the standing, dark-haired apostles are looking. Presumably they are watching Christ wash Peter's feet, but their gaze is poorly aimed. These figures have been shifted from a more logical position in an earlier version, which must have allowed them to look at what they were supposed to see. To regain that earlier version, we must move them to the right of Peter. The lower parts of their bodies, omitted out of regard for the figure and action of Christ, will of course have to be supplied. The white-haired John and Andrew, on the left, may then move to a point behind Peter. This correction expands the composition to the right, where there is no room. The prototype was a frieze broader than could be accommodated on this page. Something has also gone wrong in the miniature of the *Last Supper*. Note the apostles seated between Judas and the reclining Peter. The angle of their heads suggests a less-than-perfect transcription from some prototype.

The "corrections" we have proposed for the Rossano *Washing of the Feet* can be seen in the eleventh-century fresco of the same subject in Sant'Angelo in Formis, (figs. 9 and 11).[23] There five apostles stand behind and to the right of Peter. Two of these look directly at the action, their heads tilted forward like the two in the foreground of the corresponding group in the Rossano miniature. The others stand behind and to the left of Christ, clearing the center of the composition for the action itself. To the left of this scene, the Sant'Angelo painter

23. E. Dobbert, *Über den Styl Niccolo Pisano's und dessen Ursprung* (Munich, 1873), p. 27. Idem, "Zur Byzantinischen Frage. Die Wandgemälde in S. Angelo in Formis," *Jahrbuch der Königlich Preussischen Kunstsammlungen* 15 (1894), pp. 125ff., 211ff. A. Venturi, *Storia dell'arte italiana*, vol. 2 (Milan, 1902), p. 371f. E. Bertaux, *L'art dans l'Italie méridionale* (Paris, 1903), p. 258.

Fig. 7. Parable of the Ten Virgins, Rossano Gospels, fol. 2v

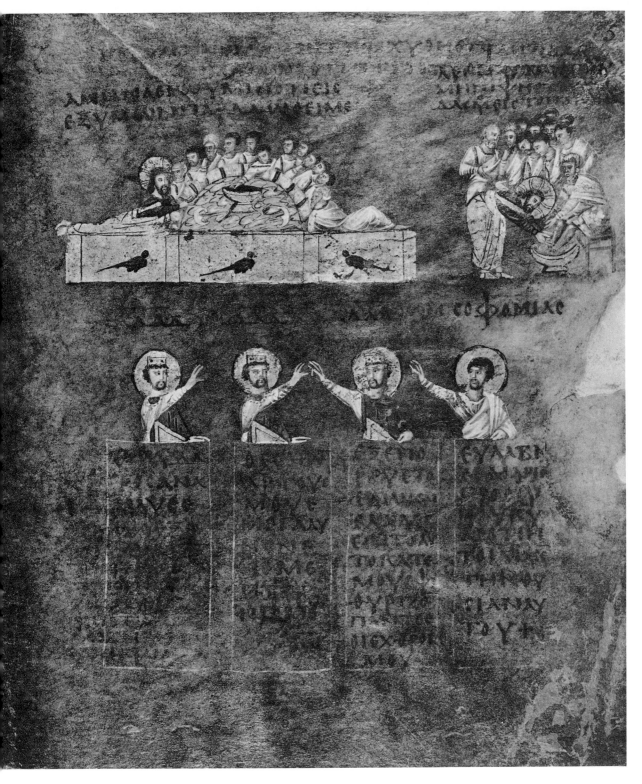

Fig. 8. Last Supper and Washing of the Feet, Rossano Gospels, fol. 3r

Fig. 9. Last Supper and Washing of the Feet. Sant'Angelo in Formis. Fresco

presented the *Last Supper* (fig. 10) in its Early Christian form, where Christ and the twelve apostles recline around a semicircular, Late Antique "sigma" table, as in the Rossano miniature. In the wall painting, however, the figure of Peter has been copied, with minor adjustments, from the *Washing of the Feet* (fig. 11). He thus strikes a rather eleventh-century note, seated as he is upon a wooden stool in front of the table. His neighbor has fallen heir to Peter's Early Christian, reclining torso, a torso virtually identical with Peter's in the Rossano miniature.

To these correspondences in detail between fresco and miniature we must add two broader observations, which will place these frescoes in an Early Christian framework known also to the Rossano miniaturist. The first is that the representations of the Last Supper and Washing of the Feet at Sant'Angelo were set side by side within a single frame.[24] Both cycles in this instance follow the liturgy in which the respective texts in Matthew and John were read in immediate succession. The second point concerns the Prophets in the spandrels of the nave arcade, who perform the same function as the Prophets below the Rossano miniatures. Eleven of the eighteen prophecies have been read and published, not without

24. F. X. Kraus, "Die Wandgemälde von S. Angelo in Formis," *Jahrbuch der Königlich Preussischen Kunstsammlungen* 14 (1893), p. 90.

Fig. 10. Last Supper (detail of fig. 9)

Fig. 11. Washing of the Feet (detail of fig. 9)

errors.[25] These are sufficient to show that the verses bear specific reference to scenes on the wall directly above them.[26] The eighteen spandrels in the nave of Sant'Angelo in Formis were used to present a prophetic text whose fulfillment could be seen directly above it. The grand cycle of the Life of Christ in this nave consisted of sixty scenes, within which it is possible to identify a liturgical *Concordia veteris et novi testamenti*. This close correspondence in detail and setting between the eleventh-century fresco and the sixth-century miniature at the least shows clearly how the compositions of the latter improve through translation onto a wall. The move from flat page to flat wall, however, involves only a shift in scale. There are no dislocations to show that one must necessarily be prior to the other.

On the Rossano page, the two scenes could not be accommodated without a cramping dislocation in the *Washing of the Feet*. One could explain this awkward compression by assuming that the miniaturist, compelled to fit two scenes of about equal breadth onto one page, took one from an illustrated Matthew, the other from an illustrated John, and did the best he could. We must remember, however, that the reason for doing this was liturgical. The resulting page is appropriate for a Lectionary, not for a Gospel book. We return to the question, why does this liturgical composition appear in a Gospel book? Was this sumptuous manuscript of purple parchment and gold and silver text made to lie on the altar in lieu of a Lectionary? Were its miniatures meant to record a monumental liturgical cycle on the walls of some basilica? The texts on this page tie it closely to the liturgy. The visual evidence in the miniature proves it to be a copy. This visual evidence, however, is insufficient to distinguish between two possible prototypes: an earlier miniature or an earlier wall painting. To decide this point, we must turn to the next miniatures in the Rossano Gospels—the *Communion of the Apostles* on folios 3v and 4r.

Scarcely anyone, it seems, has ever doubted that the *Communion of the Apostles* in the Rossano Gospels derived from a monumental prototype. The broad spacing of the figures, the unique use of two pages for one scene with the resulting grand, frieze-like file of apostles, the substantial number of wall paintings in the apses of

25. A. Moppert-Schmidt, *Die Fresken von S. Angelo in Formis* (Zürich, 1967), p. 23f. O. Morisani, *Gli affreschi di S. Angelo in Formis* (Naples, 1962), p. 85f.

26. On the north wall, six legible verses apply to scenes of the Passion cycle in the first register immediately above the spandrels. On the south wall, four of the five legible verses apply to scenes of the lost, but identified, Nativity cycle in the top register between the clerestory windows. The fifth verse (Zachariah 9:10) applies to the *Entry into Jerusalem*, set directly above the Prophet; see Appendix 2 of Morisani, *Gli affreschi*, with the numbered elevations at the end of the book.

later Byzantine churches showing the same composition—all this signaled to the earliest students of this manuscript that these miniatures copied a wall painting. What remains to be done is to clarify the relation between these miniatures and their prototype and to suggest its birthplace.

When we open the book to folios 3v and 4r, the Communion scene lies spread before us across two pages (figs. 12 and 13). At first glance this appears to be a centralized composition appropriate to its subject, the Distribution of Bread, on the left, and Wine, on the right, to two files of six apostles each. Yet something has clearly gone awry. The two files are moving in opposite directions and yet presumably reach the same altar, though no altar is shown. There is a simple way to restore spatial logic. Pick up each margin and bring them almost together, forming a cylinder with the two pages. This action positions the two figures of Christ back to back, allowing sufficient space to place an altar between them. To this altar the two files of apostles now move from right and left. This is, of course, no way to look at a book; yet by this simple action we have re-created the centralized composition followed by the miniaturist. We have re-created the original composition, but we have not yet defined the spectator's view of it. We must place ourselves inside the cylinder, our back to the binding of the book, looking directly ahead to the two figures of Christ. We now realize that the Wine is on the spectator's left and the Bread on his right. This must have been the arrangement in the monumental setting of the prototype—i.e., in the drum of a dome or in the horizontal band of an apse.

The miniaturist could have recalled the original more closely by reversing the order of these pages and placing the two figures of Christ back to back at the binding. Perhaps he had a reason for wishing to keep the Bread on the left and the Wine on the right, an order followed in at least eighty percent of the extant versions of this composition. The prototype, however, must have had the Wine on the left and the Bread on the right.

The fundamental point of the Communion of the Apostles is to demonstrate clearly and distinctly the two elements of the Sacrament: the Bread and the Wine. The subject therefore demands a central composition focused on the altar, where Christ, depicted twice to serve as two deacons, distributes Bread and Wine to two groups of apostles approaching opposite sides of the altar. With requirements as clear as these, it would not be surprising if similar compositions came independently into existence. Similar compositions, therefore, do not prove common origin. To identify scenes related to the prototypes of the Rossano miniatures, we need to bear in mind the following distinctive features of these miniatures: the apostles approach in a carefully spaced file, heads bent forward in deference; they bow low to receive the Sacrament and may raise their arms in exaltation afterwards; an occasional figure will approach with hands covered; all concentrate on the Sacrament; there is no discussion or wayward movement.

Two early witnesses to this Communion scene have been recognized in the well-known liturgical patens of the sixth century: the Stuma paten in the Archaeological Museum, Istanbul (fig. 14), and the Riha paten at Dumbarton Oaks (fig.

Fig. 12. Communion of the Apostles: Distribution of Bread. Rossano Gospels, fol. 3v

Fig. 13. Communion of the Apostles: Distribution of Wine. Rossano Gospels, fol. 4r

William C. Loerke

Fig. 14. Stuma paten. Istanbul, Archaeological Museum, Silver gilt

15).[27] The compositions on these patens supply the altar omitted in the Rossano miniatures. They also show the Wine on the left and the Bread on the right, as in the Rossano prototype. However, the round format in these compositions has made it impossible for the silversmiths to present the apostles in single-file procession as in the Rossano miniatures. There does, however, survive on each plate a remnant of the original procession in the two leading apostles of each group. On each plate only the first two apostles to receive the Bread and Wine are shown in single file and they alone concentrate on the Sacrament. Behind these apostles are clustered four figures on each side of the altar who in the Stuma paten (fig. 14) stare out at the observer as rather uninvolved attendants; one of them raises his right hand in witness to a theophany.

The Stuma silversmith has followed the Rossano prototype as far as space permitted. This is clear from the fact that the two leading figures of each group

27. M. Ross, *Catalogue of the Byzantine and Early Medieval Antiquities in the Dumbarton Oaks Collection*, I. *Metalwork, Ceramics, Glass, Glyptics, Painting* (Washington, D.C., 1962), pp. 12ff. E. Cruikshank Dodd, *Byzantine Silver Stamps* (Washington, D.C., 1961), pp. 95, 108.

Fig. 15. Riha paten. Washington, D.C., Dumbarton Oaks. Silver gilt

are the only ones that can be closely matched in the Rossano miniatures. The figure
on the extreme left with upraised arms has a close parallel in the apostle immediately behind the one receiving the Bread on fol. 3v. The bowed figure in front
of the altar repeats the posture of the apostles actually receiving the Sacrament in
the Rossano miniatures. This figure is clearly misplaced, for he has passed the
point of reception though his posture indicates he is approaching the altar. This
entire group should be moved to the right, in order to place the bowed apostle
at Christ's hand. In adapting the original composition to his circular frame the
Stuma silversmith faced a much more difficult task than the Rossano miniaturist.
He captured the rhythm of a procession only in the first figures of each group and
these alone are shown in profile. The remaining four figures of each group had

to be shown behind the first two, and these, while overlapped in sequence, still are shown frontally rather than in profile.

The artist of the Riha paten placed a ground line under the scene, schematically indicated a sanctuary behind it, and reduced the height and breadth of the altar. He too was able to preserve the first two figures of each original file, though the second one crowds too closely on the first in each case. The figures are better scaled to the restricted setting, and a greater concentration upon the Sacrament has been maintained. The stamps on the reverse of these plates argue for Constantinople as their place of manufacture, attesting to knowledge of the prototype there in the second half of the sixth century.

At this point the Iconoclastic Controversy breaks the tradition. When we pick up the trail of the Rossano version in post-Iconoclastic Byzantine art, the representations closest to the miniatures are to be found only in monumental wall painting, particularly of the eleventh century. Post-Iconoclastic miniatures of the Communion, on the other hand, follow more nearly the lead of the silver plates, particularly in bunching the apostles into two groups, rather than spacing them broadly in two files. This is the case in the Constantinopolitan Psalters. The Chloudov Psalter (fig. 16) places directly behind the altar a single Christ, who administers the Bread to Peter, first of a group of bowing apostles on the left; Christ rather ignores the other group on the right, whose leader takes the chalice in his own hands.[28] The scene is flanked by David, left, and Melchisedek, right, in response to its position with Psalm 109, verse 4 of which reads "Thou art a priest forever after the order of Melchisedek." The application to Christ of this messianic prophecy was developed at great length by the writer of Hebrews, chapters 7 and 8. A Mount Athos Psalter in Pantokratoros (fig. 17), dating from the second half of the ninth century, follows the same iconography, but the scene is placed at Psalm 33, verse 9, which says, "Taste and see that the Lord is good."[29] This is also the first verse under the Distribution of the Bread in the Rossano Gospels, whose liturgical significance we shall examine later.

Of the famous Psalters of the eleventh century, both the Barberini (fig. 18) and the Theodore (fig. 19) follow the lead of the Chloudov Psalter in placing the Communion scene at Psalm 109.[30] Christ, turned to the left, administers the

28. N. V. Malitzky, "Traits d'iconographie palestinienne dans le psautier byzantin à illustrations marginales du type Chloudoff" (in Russian), *Seminarium Kondakovianum*, vol. 1 (1927), p. 57 and pl. 5, fig. 1.

29. S. Dufrenne, *L'illustration des psautiers grecs du Moyen Age*, I: *Pantocrator 61, Paris grec 20, British Museum add. 40731* (Paris, 1966), p. 24 and pl. 5.

30. The Barberini Psalter is, as yet, unpublished. For the Theodore Psalter, see S. Der Nersessian, *L'illustration des psautiers grecs du Moyen Age*, II: *Londres, Add. 19.352* (Paris, 1970), p. 52 and pl. 89, fig. 244.

Fig. 16. Communion of the Apostles. Moscow, Historical Museum, cod. 129 (Chloudov Psalter), fol. 111

Fig. 17. Communion of the Apostles. Mount Athos, Pantokratoros, cod. 61

Fig. 18. Communion of the Apostles. Rome, Vatican Library, cod. Barb. gr. 372 (Barberini Psalter), fol. 188r

Fig. 19. Communion of the Apostles. London, British Museum, cod. add. 19352 (Theodore Psalter), fol. 152r

Bread to Peter, at the head of a cluster of six apostles, while the leading figure of the right-hand group drinks from a chalice he himself holds. The Barberini and the Theodore Psalter versions have also retained, like the Chloudov, the prophetic figures in the margin, David on the left and Melchisedek on the right. The Bristol Psalter follows the example of the Mount Athos Psalter in assigning its Communion scene to Psalm 33.[31] Here a frontal Christ, standing behind the altar, raises his right hand in blessing.

The Communion scene in the scroll with the Liturgy of John Chrysostom in Jerusalem (fig. 20) is more formal and hieratic in character than the Psalter illustrations just mentioned.[32] A frontal Christ raises his right hand in blessing behind an altar flanked by angels holding *flabella*. The apostles, bending forward, approach in two groups led on the left by Peter and on the right by Paul. In each margin outside the twisted vine frame stands an additional angel, drawn to a larger scale than those in the scene itself. This miniature, far more carefully composed than those in the Psalters, conveys a sense of balanced order and intense concentration reminiscent of the Rossano composition. This effect is achieved however, through the symmetrical positioning of the angels and groups of apostles flanking the central altar, rather than by broad and monumental spacing of individual figures as in the Rossano miniatures.

The liturgical aura present in varying degrees in all these miniatures has lost much of its intensity in the Communion miniature in the late-eleventh-century Gospels in Paris (fig. 21).[33] This miniaturist seems out of touch with the prototype we seek, even though he shows Christ twice to administer both Bread and Wine, and presents the apostles in single, though crowded file. The space available and the scale to which he drew his figures offered ample space in which to spread out the broad original composition, a composition that he must have known but in which he had little interest. The scene is pointlessly set in a landscape and casually composed with the altar off-center. There are only five apostles in the left group and four in the right, about half of whom turn their heads and attention away from the altar. None bows or bends forward in deference to the Sacrament, nor do any exhibit the haste or intensity of the Rossano apostles. A vital force has left the composition.

Full and substantial witnesses to the prototype of the Rossano miniatures are to be found only in monumental painting of the eleventh century, specifically in the apses of two churches dedicated to Saint Sophia, in fresco at Ohrid (fig. 22) and in mosaic at Kiev (fig. 23). Broad spacing of figures, none overlapped; serious concentration in every figure: these are the hallmarks of the prototype. In the fresco at Ohrid, the concentration of the apostles is almost fierce; all except

---

31. Dufrenne, *Illustration*, p. 57 and pl. 50.

32. A. Grabar, "Un rouleau liturgique constantinopolitain et ses peintures," *Dumbarton Oaks Papers* 8 (1954), p. 174 and fig. 10.

33. H. Omont, *Evangiles avec peintures byzantines du XIᵉ siècle*, vol. 2 (Paris, n.d.), pl. 133.

Fig. 20. Communion of the Apostles. Jerusalem, Greek Patriarchate, cod. Staurou 109, R12

Fig. 21. Communion of the Apostles. Paris, Bibliothèque Nationale, cod. gr. 74, fol. 156v

Peter approach with covered hands.[34] In the mosaic at Kiev, classic restraint and serenity is the rule, which tells us that here we stand stylistically closer to the prototype than in Ohrid. Kiev is also closer to the prototype compositionally, for the grander dimensions of that Hagia Sophia permitted the mosaicist a broad altar flanked by angels and a doubled figure of Christ, striding forward to administer both the Bread and the Wine to the two files of approaching apostles.[35] The smaller dimensions of Saint Sophia, Ohrid, compelled the painter, in the interest of presenting the full, uncrowded procession, to restrict the size of the altar, to place attendant angels behind the leading apostles, and to be content with a single frontal Christ standing behind the altar, blessing the faithful in the church rather than administering the Sacrament to the apostles.

Examination of these two monumental versions of the Rossano prototype makes it clear why the Rossano miniaturist needed two pages for his composition (figs. 12 and 13). Even with two pages available, he still had to choose between the solemn, hieratic procession of apostles, or the altar; he could not have both. Miniaturists who chose the altar had to give up the procession. No other Gospel scene requires a lateral expanse so disproportionate to its height. Clearly this broad, frieze-like composition of the Communion did not originate on the rectangular page of a Gospel book. Its peculiar ratio between breadth and height, its centripetal focus, the supreme importance of the altar—these characteristics point to a horizontal band in the apse, the soffit of a broad arch, or the drum of a dome as its physical birthplace.

To summarize: The Rossano miniatures of the Communion report the existence by the sixth century of a monumental composition of the Communion to which the silver patens from Syria bear a variant witness. This witness continues in Constantinopolitan Psalters of the ninth and eleventh centuries. The key monuments that give us an idea of its full size are the fresco and mosaic in the apses of the two Saint Sophias, in Ohrid and in Kiev. This recital of witnesses indicates the key role played by Constantinople in the transmission of this famous composition. Let me briefly suggest a monument in Constantinople that could have played this role.

In the symposium at Dumbarton Oaks mentioned at the outset of this paper, Professor Friend described the lost mosaic program of the Holy Apostles' Church, Constantinople, as the pictorial answer to Iconoclasm. He concluded his argument by stressing the importance of the Communion scene as the theological capstone of the program. The mosaic of the Communion, set over the altar on the soffit of the great eastern arch, was described by Mesarites as follows: "Christ himself stands at the table as though at an altar. For an altar indeed is this holy and mystic table. . . . He sheds his blood into the cup which he holds in front of himself

34. R. Hamann-Mac Lean and H. Hallensleben, *Die Monumentalmalerei in Serbien und Makedonien. Bildband* (Giessen, 1963), figs. 4 and 6.

35. H. Logvin, *Kiev's Hagia Sophia* (Kiev, 1971), pls. 51–68.

Fig. 22. Communion of the Apostles. Ohrid, Saint Sophia, apse. Fresco

Fig. 23. Communion of the Apostles. Kiev, Saint Sophia, apse. Mosaic

with his hands. And he gives them to eat of his flesh. . . ."[36] Since Christ in this mosaic holds the cup with his hands and also distributes the Bread, he must have been represented twice, in a composition like those we have been examining. This must have been the major version of this scene in Constantinople. I suggest that it was the chief intermediary link between Kiev and Ohrid, on the one hand, and the monumental prototype of the Rossano miniatures, on the other.

The theological importance of the Communion with respect to Iconoclasm is that its representation refutes one of the major contentions of the Iconoclasts, i.e., that the only symbols Christ gave of his body were the Bread and the Wine. This could be refuted by pointing to the words of Institution, which do not say "Take, eat, this is the symbol of my body," but rather, "Take, eat, this is my body." To represent Christ distributing the Bread and the Wine was to affirm at once the Incarnation and the mystic Communion. The inscription over the Rossano miniatures stresses this point, but does so in a way that leads me to believe that it may reproduce the inscription on the monumental prototype.

The uncial inscription above the Distribution of the Bread on fol. 3v reads, "taking bread, having given thanks, he gave to them saying, This is my body" (ΛΑΒωΝ ΑΡΤΟΝ ΕVΧΑΡΙCΤΗCΑC ΕΔωΚΕΝ ΑVΤΟΙC ΛΕΓωΝ ΤΟVΤΟ ΕCΤΙΝ ΤΟ CωΜΑ ΜΟV). Over the Wine on folio 4r we read, "taking the cup, having given thanks, he gave to them saying, This is my blood" (ΛΑΒωΝ ΠΟΤΗΡΙΟΝ ΕVΧΑΡΙCΤΗCΑC ΕΔωΚΕΝ ΑVΤΟΙC ΛΕΓωΝ ΤΟVΤΟ ΕCΤΙΝ ΤΟ ΑΙΜΑ ΜΟV).[37] In Greek, there are eleven words in each inscription, with "cup" and "blood" in the second substituting for "bread" and "body" in the first. The rigorous parallelism of these statements cannot be matched in the New Testament accounts of the Institution of the Eucharist.

When we compare these texts with their four possible sources in the New Testament, the texts of Matthew 26:26f., Mark 14:22f., Luke 22:19f., and I Corinthians 11:23f., we find that the first inscription matches most closely the version given by Luke. One word, however, ἔκλασεν ("he broke it,") has dropped out, though it is present in all four sources. The second inscription does not follow Luke or Paul but most closely matches the text of Matthew. In this case a whole phrase has been omitted, πίετε ἐξ αὐτοῦ πάντες ("Drink ye all of it"). The tight parallelism of these inscriptions was achieved first by selecting the most concise of the four available sources, and then by suppressing those verbs that could not apply to both elements, the Bread and the Wine.

These inscriptions are unique among those appearing above miniatures in the Rossano Gospels. The other inscriptions fall into one of two types: either a

36. Nikolaos Mesarites, "Description of the Church of the Holy Apostles at Constantinople," ed. and transl. G. Downey, in *Transactions of the American Philosophical Society*, n.s. 47, part 6 (Philadelphia, 1957), p. 871.

37. Muñoz, *Codice purpureo*, p. 4.

Gospel verse correctly quoted, as above the *Last Supper* and above the *Washing of the Feet* on folio 3r; or a chapter heading, as over the *Parable of the Virgins*, where we read, "Concerning the ten virgins."

Students of the Eucharistic words agree that a liturgical desire for parallel statements about the Bread and the Wine already affected the Gospel texts themselves, but not to the point of dropping the words omitted in the Rossano inscriptions.[38] In later practice, one can find instances where ἔκλασεν is omitted, but the result never achieves the severe parallelism of the Rossano version.[39] The closest parallel to the spirit and form of these inscriptions I find in the beginning of the Fourth Mystagogical Lecture of Cyril of Jerusalem. He opened this lecture on the Eucharist by quoting the Pauline account. However, when he came to the words of Institution themselves, consciously or not, he substituted his own liturgical practice for the words of Paul. He added phrases from Matthew 26:26 with respect to the Bread; like the Rossano inscription, he departed entirely from the Lucan-Pauline tradition with respect to the Wine, giving instead his own liturgical version of Matthew 26:27 (for the texts, see the Appendix). Clearly, the Rossano inscriptions are not straightforward Biblical quotations. They derive from liturgical practice, but surpass known liturgical practice in their concise, spare balance. For this reason they may be the faithful copies of monumental originals, whose visual demand for concise, symmetrical statements was greater than the aural demand for the same in the liturgy itself.

Liturgical practice has left its mark on these pages most plainly in the first of the Old Testament verses of folio 3r, below the Distribution of the Bread. This verse is Psalm 33:9: "Taste and see that the Lord is good." The Apostolic Constitutions prescribe this Psalm to be sung while the faithful partake of the Sacrament.[40] That this was the practice in Jerusalem is clear from Cyril's description of the Eucharistic rite, where he mentions the chanter, "with sacred melody inviting you to the communion of the Holy Mysteries and saying, 'O taste and see that the Lord is good'."[41] Indeed, the haste of the apostles' approach for the Bread, and the ecstasy of the one who has received it are best described in verse 6 of Psalm 33: "Hasten to him and be enlightened."[42] The visual-verbal continuum we noted between inscription and pictured action on folio 3r (*Last Supper* and *Washing of the Feet*) makes it plausible to see this Communion miniature as a visual

38. H. Lietzmann, *Mass and Lord's Supper*, transl. D. H. Reeve, with Introduction and Supplementary Essay by R. D. Richardson, (Leiden, fasc. 1–4, 1953–1955), p. 179. J. Jeremias, *The Eucharistic Words of Christ* (Oxford, 1955), pp. 101ff.

39. Lietzmann, *Mass*, pp. 233, 237.

40. *Apostolic Constitutions* VIII, 13.

41. Cyril of Jerusalem, *Mystagogical Catechesis* V, 20.

42. For the association of these verses with the community of the enlightened as described in the Letter to the Hebrews and in I Peter, see Hans Kosmala, *Hebräer-Essener-Christen* (Leiden, 1959), pp. 122ff.

William C. Loerke

statement of Psalm 33:6, while the end and aim of this approach is written out below in verse 8.

Our search for the prototype of the Rossano *Communion of the Apostles* has led us to describe a monumental composition that could have been seen on the walls of a prominent basilica by the mid-sixth century. Certain liturgical data have already led us to Jerusalem, making it appropriate to inquire whether the original we seek had been set in the very structure that commemorated the event—the Coenaculum in Sion Church. The "upper room" of Mark 14:15 and Luke 22:12 (ἀνάγαιον μέγα ἐστρωμένον) had become the "upper church of the apostles" by the mid-fourth century for the auditors of Cyril of Jerusalem.[43] At the end of the century, Aetheria attended services there commemorating the post-Resurrection appearances of Christ to the disciples and the descent of the Spirit at Pentecost.[44] In her day, the Maundy Thursday Communion service took place behind the Cross on Golgotha;[45] but by the mid-fifth century, according to the Old Armenian Lectionary,[46] the service then continued in Sion.

An Armenian description of the Holy Places, written in the seventh century, contains the oldest reference to a painting in this room: "To the right of the Church (Sion), the chamber of the mysteries, and a wooden cupola in which is imaged the sacred supper of the Saviour. In it an altar at which the liturgy is celebrated."[47] It is difficult to imagine how the historical Last Supper, with Christ and the apostles reclining around a single table, could be fitted into a dome. The *Communion of the Apostles*, however, with its double procession, can easily occupy such a space, as the frescoes in the church of Saint Nicholas at Demre-Myra prove.[48] Additional paintings were added or at least seen and recorded subsequently. The monk Epiphanius (twelfth century[?]) saw a painting of the Pharisee and the Publican in the Coenaculum.[49] Also in the twelfth century, John of Würzburg recorded a mosaic of the *Pentecost* event in an apse, the *Last Supper* in the upper church, and the *Washing of the Feet* in the crypt.[50] The early reference to the wooden cupola with its painting, however, reminds us to take a closer look at the two silver patens because they are the only pre-Iconoclastic examples of this scene that give an indication of the setting (figs. 14 and 15).

43. Cyril of Jerusalem, *Cathechesis* 16, 4: "ἐν τῇ τῶν ἀποστόλων 'εκκλησία,'" Migne, *P.G.* 33, col. 924.

44. *Peregrinatio Aetheriae*, 39, 43.

45. Ibid., 35.

46. Conybeare, *Rituale Armenorum*, p. 520.

47. R. N. Bain, "Armenian Description of the Holy Places in the Seventh Century," *Palestine Exploration Fund Quarterly* (1896), p. 347.

48. I owe this reference to Cyril Mango.

49. Epiphanius Monachus, *Enarratio Syriae*, in Migne, *P.G.*, 120, col. 261.

50. T. Tobler, *Descriptiones Terrae Sanctae* (Leipzig, 1874), pp. 136, 147, and 157.

The artist of the Riha paten at Dumbarton Oaks shows us a segment of a trabeate chancel screen, supported by spiral fluted columns, only two of which could be represented in the meager space available between the figures. Above each column sits a lamp, and the center is marked by an arch, containing a shell motif. These elements constitute adequate artistic shorthand for a trabeate chancel screen that extended beyond the limits imposed by the circular dish, and whose central intercolumniation would be spanned by an arch.[51] The shell within the arch may be read verbally, yielding κόγχη, a word that denotes, in addition to "shell," the quarter-sphere or conch of an apse. Thus the Riha paten shows us the altar in its basilical setting.

In the Stuma paten in Istanbul, on the contrary, a crescent-shaped element rises directly from the two halos of the doubled figures of Christ. A lamp is suspended from the center of this, while a cone-like finial marks its crown. No supporting columns are shown, though the artist could have found space to show their upper parts had he extended the diameter of this domical structure beyond the heads of the two Christs. One should not, therefore, leap immediately to the conclusion that a ciborium is intended. The upper surface of the dome has striations that may represent grass or foliage, such as we find on certain domes or aediculas in the miniatures of the Rabula Gospels (folios 1 and 14). The Stuma artist could be telling us that his Communion scene was located in or transpiring under a dome. Thus our three earliest representations of the prototype provide complementary data, all of which harmonize with the early Armenian description of the "upper room." The Rossano miniatures provide the full hieratic procession of the apostles, the Riha paten presents the altar and chancel screen, and the Stuma paten adds the dome.

Ten pages of the Rossano, including the Communion scene, show four figures of Old Testament Prophets below the miniatures of scenes from the Life of Christ. Their verses make specific and concrete reference not only to the miniature as a whole, but to that part of the miniature to which the author points. We must therefore speak of these pages as full-page miniatures in which the Old Testament in word confronts the New in image. The specific and concrete reference of verse to pictured event is identical with the use of Old Testament verses in Matthew's Gospel and with the juxtaposition of these verses to Gospel lections in the early liturgy of Jerusalem. Aetheria's account of Holy Week services in Jerusalem constantly speaks of readings, prayers, and hymns, i.e., psalms, "apt to the day and place." The specific identification of a place where a theophany occurred, i.e., a *locus sanctus*, focused the mind concretely on the event, led to its celebration in a liturgy that carefully selected and integrated readings of the Old and New Testament, and led also to the careful depiction of the event, so that the event

51. For other examples, see S. Xydis, "The Chancel Barrier, Solia, and Ambo of Hagia Sophia," *Art Bulletin* 29 (1947), pp. 1–11.

would remain in that place on the wall as a visible deed when the liturgy fell silent.

Seeing the deeds of Christ as the fulfillment of prophecy began with Christ himself in the Gospels. In John 5:39 he had said, "Search the scriptures (i.e., the Old Testament), for they testify of me." On the walk to Emmaus, he upbraided two disciples for not believing what the Prophets said and beginning with Moses, "he went through all the prophets and explained all the scriptures concerning himself" (Luke 24:27). In his final appearance he reminded them that everything "written in the law of Moses, in the prophets and in the psalms concerning me" (Luke 24:44) had to be fulfilled. Peter's first sermon (Acts 1:16ff.) began on precisely this point. The "dialogue" between the Life of Christ and the scriptures was thus launched even before Pentecost and continued unabated in the Apostolic age. It drew its sustenance from an audience of Jews who knew and accepted the Prophets and Psalms, but had to be convinced of their application to the Life of Christ. The public relevance of this scriptural view of the Life of Christ would continue when and where there was such an audience to be addressed. It is not accidental, therefore, that the liturgy of Jerusalem, as we can know it from Aetheria's account and from the old Armenian and Georgian liturgies, should be the oldest public vehicle for this dialogue between the deeds of Christ and the words of prophecy.[52] It is that liturgical practice that has formed the pages of the Rossano Gospels we have been studying.

A further point was made by confronting the Life of Christ in pictures with the written text of prophecy. The Church Fathers and Byzantine writers followed ancient theory in elevating pictures above words, because sight was believed to be more persuasive and convincing than hearing. Pictures bring deeds vividly before us, without the intervention of words, transforming the auditor of a text into an eyewitness of a deed.[53] In this context, the miniatures and their monumental prototypes counted as deeds in contrast to the words below them. This contrast precisely matched an Early Christian typology that equated the Old Testament with words and the New with deeds.[54] Thus, pictures of the Life of Christ set on the walls of a basilica were not only the Bible of the illiterate. They stood as the very deeds that fulfilled the words of prophetic scripture. The miniatures of the Rossano Gospels record this typology as the Church taught it to the faithful in the public liturgy of Jerusalem.

52. In the twelfth century, John of Würzburg was shown, in the upper part of the church at Calvary, a beautiful mosaic containing "the passion of Christ and his burial along with the witness of the prophets agreeing on this side and on that with the deed shown" (Tobler, *Descriptiones*, p. 144).

53. Nicephorus, *Antirrheticus III Adv. Constantinum Copronymum*, 3 and 5; Migne, *P.G.*, 100, 380D and 381D.

54. H. de Lubac, *Exegèse médiévale: les quatre sens de l'Ecriture*, vol. 1 (Paris, 1959), pp. 305ff.

In the texts below, I underline those words that appear in the inscriptions over the Communion miniatures of the Rossano Gospels:

Cyril of Jerusalem, Mystagogical *Cathechesis* IV, I ("quoting" I Cor. 11: 23–25)

I Cor. 11: 23–25

ὅτι ἐν τῇ νυκτὶ ᾗ παρεδίδοτο ὁ κύριος ἡμῶν Ἰησοῦς Χριστός, λαβὼν ἄρτον καὶ εὐχαριστήσας ἔκλασε καὶ ἔδωκε τοῖς ἑαυτοῦ μαθηταῖς[1] λέγων· λάβετε,[2] φάγετε,[3] τοῦτό μού ἐστι τὸ σῶμα.

. . . ὅτι ὁ κύριος Ἰησοῦς ἐν τῇ νυκτὶ ᾗ παρεδίδοτο ἔλαβεν ἄρτον καὶ εὐχαριστήσας ἔκλασεν καὶ εἶπεν,

τοῦτό μού ἐστι τὸ σῶμα τὸ ὑπὲρ ὑμῶν· τοῦτο ποιεῖτε εἰς τὴν ἐμὴν ἀνάμνησιν.

καὶ λαβὼν τὸ ποτήριον καὶ εὐχαριστήσας εἶπε· λάβετε,[4] πίετε,[5] τοῦτό μού ἐστι τὸ αἷμα.[6]

ὡσαύτως καὶ τὸ ποτήριον μετὰ τὸ δειπνῆσαι λέγων· τοῦτο τὸ ποτήριον ἡ καινὴ διαθήκη ἐστὶν ἐν τῷ ἐμῷ αἵματι.

1–3.   From Matt. 26:26
4.   Repeated from Matt. 26:26 for the sake of parallelism
5–6.   From Matt. 26:27

Ernst Kitzinger

The Role of Miniature Painting in Mural Decoration

Parva ex magnis might have been the title of William Loerke's paper. *Magna ex parvis* could be a complementary title for mine. I shall undertake to explore the role of miniatures in mural decoration. And I must start with an emphatic disclaimer. The subject is vast. It could not be encompassed in a short essay even if I had the competence to deal comprehensively with all its aspects. Nor have I any startling revelations to offer. I have not discovered any hitherto unnoticed connections between an illuminated manuscript and a monumental decoration, any new link like the famous one between the Cotton Genesis and the mosaics in the vestibule of San Marco in Venice. What I have to say will be in the nature of observations, comments, and suggestions. Intended as a tribute to the scholar who has done more than anyone else in our time to advance our knowledge and understanding of the history of book illustration, they are also meant to promote discussion of a complex problem.[1]

I have mentioned the Old Testament cycle in San Marco. It is the classic case—the example any historian of medieval art immediately thinks of—when the notion of miniatures as a basis for wall decoration is brought up for discussion. Because it occupies such a prominent role in relation to my subject, I propose to turn to it first.

1. Warm thanks are due to Kurt Weitzmann for his help in preparing this paper for publication. He has been generous in answering queries I put to him and has provided a number of the photographs used in the illustrations. For the prints reproduced as fig. 30 and fig. 31 I am indebted to Professor L. Budde, Münster, and Dr. I. Nikolajević, Belgrad, respectively. The paper in its final form was completed in December 1973.

As everyone knows, it was J. J. Tikkanen who discovered the close relationship between the thirteenth-century cycle of scenes from Genesis in San Marco and the miniatures of the fifth–sixth-century Bible in the British Museum once owned by Sir Robert Cotton. Having announced his essential results in an article in 1888, Tikkanen published his famous monograph in the following year.[2] I shall not rehearse the evidence marshaled by him but shall let the best-known, most legible, and most palpable of his comparisons speak for itself. The scene in question is the Third Day of Creation (fig. 1). To illustrate its manuscript prototype we need not use the half-charred remains of the Cotton Bible itself, since there exists a copy of the miniature, made before the fire of 1731 that reduced the manuscript to the pathetic ruin that survives today (fig. 2). The comparison is one of many, equally close, that can be made between the Cotton miniatures and the Venetian mosaics.

To be sure, there are also differences. We owe to Kurt Weitzmann the fullest analysis of these.[3] Only about a third of the scenes that the manuscript must have contained appear in San Marco. Some of the scenes are conflated. Many panels differ in format. There are compositional adjustments. And although the mosaics clearly reproduce not only the iconography of the Cotton Genesis but also essential characteristics of its Late Antique style, particularly in the rendering of figures

2. J. J. Tikkanen, "Le rappresentazioni della Genesi in S. Marco a Venezia e loro relazione con la Bibbia Cottoniana," *Archivio storico dell'arte* 1 (1888), pp. 212ff., 257ff., 348ff. Idem, *Die Genesismosaiken von S. Marco in Venedig und ihr Verhältniss zu den Miniaturen der Cottonbibel*, Acta Societatis Scientiarum Fennicae, vol. 17 (Helsingfors, 1889; reprinted Soest, 1972).

3. K. Weitzmann, "Observations on the Cotton Genesis Fragments," *Late Classical and Mediaeval Studies in Honor of Albert Mathias Friend, Jr.* (Princeton, 1955), pp. 112ff., especially pp. 119ff. Idem, "The Mosaics of San Marco and the Cotton Genesis," *Atti del XVIII Congresso Internazionale di Storia dell'Arte, Venezia 12–18 Settembre 1955* (Venice, 1956), p. 152f. See also G. Henderson, "Late Antique Influences in some English Mediaeval Illustrations of Genesis," *Journal of the Warburg and Courtauld Institutes* 25 (1962), pp. 172ff., especially pp. 178ff., 183ff. Sahoko Tsuji, "La chaire de Maximien, la Genèse de Cotton et les mosaiques de Saint-Marc à Venise: à propos du cycle de Joseph," *Synthronon* (= Bibliothèque des Cahiers Archéologiques 3 [Paris, 1968]), pp. 43ff. Prof. Tsuji's claim that the artists at San Marco must have made use also of a second early manuscript that supplied models for at least two scenes in the Joseph cycle allegedly not illustrated in the Cotton Genesis is not convincing. As Kurt Weitzmann has kindly informed me, there was room for the two scenes in question on folio 73v and folio 74r respectively of the Cotton manuscript. Both these folios are heavily damaged.

Some new elements have recently been introduced into the discussion of the relationship between the Cotton Genesis and the San Marco mosaics in a study by K. Koshi, *Die Genesisminiaturen in der Wiener "Histoire universelle" (Cod. 2576)*, Wiener kunstgeschichtliche Forschungen, 1 (Vienna, 1973). This monograph became available to me only when the present article was already in proof.

Fig. 1. Third Day of Creation. Venice, San Marco, atrium, first dome. Mosaic

Fig. 2. Third Day of Creation (copy made for N. Peiresc after Cotton Genesis miniature). Paris, Bibliothèque Nationale, cod. fr. 9530, fol. 32 (after Omont)

(see figs. 3 and 4), they also show an unmistakable admixture of thirteenth-century forms. As work progressed in the five bays of the vestibule of San Marco devoted to the Book of Genesis, this stylistic transformation increased. While the essential iconography of the Cotton Genesis was retained throughout, the scenes executed in the later stages of the work—especially those in the fourth and fifth bays depicting the life of Joseph in Egypt—display much more frankly a thirteenth-century style (fig. 5).[4]

For the moment it is the close similarity between miniatures and mosaics that I want to emphasize. With extraordinary fidelity the mosaics retained the iconography[5] and in part the style of their ancient prototype. Hardly anyone has doubted this relationship;[6] we all operate with it as a given fact; and, indeed, the mosaics in turn have been used extensively to reconstruct damaged or missing illustrations in the manuscript. Tikkanen's discovery was one of those elemental breakthroughs in scholarship that will never be undone.

Art historical inquiry has not, however, stood still in the eighty-five years since the Finnish scholar wrote. To put his discovery into perspective in relation to my overall subject, I shall cite certain basic assumptions that he made in regard to the Cotton-San Marco relationship and that subsequent research, while based on his findings, has called into question. Specifically, I shall draw attention to three such assumptions: (1) that the manuscript now in the British Museum was

4. O. Demus, *Die Mosaiken von San Marco in Venedig 1100–1300* (Baden bei Wien, 1935), pp. 56ff.

5. I take this opportunity to set the record straight regarding one of the iconographic details that have been thought not to be based on the Cotton manuscript, namely, the figures personifying the Four Rivers of Paradise in the scene of Adam's Introduction into Paradise. It was erroneously claimed by E. Schlee that the Four Rivers were not represented in anthropomorphic form prior to the year A.D. 1000 (*Die Ikonographie der Paradiesesflüsse* [Leipzig, 1937], passim); and this led to the conclusion that at San Marco the four figures in question were in all probability filler motifs added by the medieval mosaicist (ibid., p. 8f.; cf. Weitzmann, "Observations," p. 127; idem, "Mosaics of San Marco," p. 153). But the Rivers of Paradise were represented in the form of human busts in a floor mosaic at Tegea, generally considered to be of the fifth century (for references, see J.-P. Sodini, in *Bulletin de Correspondance Hellénique* 94 [1970], p. 709); and on a sixth-century mosaic at Gasr el-Lebia, discovered in 1957, they are depicted in a manner strikingly similar to the representations at San Marco, namely, in the guise of reclining river gods with overturned water vessels (J. B. Ward Perkins, in *Atti del VI Congresso Internazionale di Archeologia Cristiana, Ravenna 1962* [Rome, 1965], p. 656, fig. 18; cf. A. Grabar, in *Cahiers Archéologiques* 12 [1962], pp. 135ff. and fig. 15; idem in *Bulletin de la société nationale des antiquaires de France* [1968], pp. 45ff.). Thus there is no longer any reason to doubt that these figures appeared in the Cotton miniature.

6. For a rare expression of skepticism on this point, see D. C. Winfield, in *Dumbarton Oaks Papers* 22 (1968), p. 94f.

not itself the source of the Venetian mosaics;[7] (2) that there were, in fact, a number of intermediaries (*Zwischenglieder*) between the two monuments;[8] and (3) that there is nothing unusual about this relationship because it simply bespeaks a lack of originality and inventiveness in later Byzantine art in general and a penchant to copy originals of early date.[9]

How exactly Tikkanen related his second assumption to his third is not clear. He does not elaborate on his presumed *Zwischenglieder*, and thus we do not know whether he thought of these intermediaries as being spread over the seven or eight centuries that separate the San Marco mosaics from the Cotton miniatures or whether he assumed them to be more or less contemporary either with the former or with the latter. But his general concept is clear. He assumed that there was in Byzantine art first a period of great inventiveness—the fifth and sixth centuries—that produced a number of different recensions of Old Testament illustrations including that of the Cotton manuscript; that this was followed by a period of stagnation during which these different recensions were repeated without much change; and that the San Marco cycle is simply a product of this ossification.

In the decades since Tikkanen's book appeared—and not least through the work of Kurt Weitzmann and his school—we have learned a great deal about the life of these recensions. Not only have they begun to acquire a prehistory reaching back, at least in some cases, to a quite remote past, but we also know now that on the whole they did not remain static and unchanged during the medieval period. More particularly does this apply to the recension represented by the Cotton manuscript, a recension that has been found to lie at the roots of an extraordinary variety of illustrative cycles or parts of cycles—Carolingian, South Italian, and northern Romanesque.[10] It is true that all these reflections are in Western art—this is a point to which I shall return—whereas Tikkanen thought of the rigid adherence to early models as being characteristic specifically of the mature art of Byzantium; and it was to Byzantine masters (or, in part, their

7. Tikkanen, *Genesismosaiken*, p. 116.

8. Ibid.

9. Ibid., pp. 116ff., 148.

10. W. Koehler, *Die karolingischen Miniaturen*, vol. 1: *Die Schule von Tours*, part 2 (Berlin, 1933), pp. 186ff. Weitzmann, "Observations," pp. 121ff. R. Green, "The Adam and Eve Cycle in the *Hortus Deliciarum*," *Late Classical and Mediaeval Studies* (see note 3 above), pp. 340ff. E. Kitzinger, *The Mosaics of Monreale* (Palermo, 1960), p. 60. H. Kessler, "An Eleventh Century Ivory Plaque from South Italy and the Cassinese Revival," *Jahrbuch der Berliner Museen* 8 (1966), pp. 67ff., especially pp. 78ff. Idem, "Hic Homo Formatur: The Genesis Frontispieces of the Carolingian Bibles," *Art Bulletin* 53 (1971), pp. 143ff. (where it is argued that the Genesis cycles in the Carolingian Bibles of the School of Tours reflect a stage in the development of the Cotton Genesis recension earlier than the Cotton manuscript itself). For possible reflections of the Cotton Genesis recension in English manuscript illustrations, see Henderson, "Late Antique

Fig. 3. Eve Introduced to Adam. Venice, San Marco, atrium, first dome. Mosaic

Fig. 4. Eve Introduced to Adam.
London, British Museum,
cod. Cotton Otho B.VI
(Cotton Genesis)

Fig. 5. Joseph and Potiphar's Wife. Venice, San Marco, atrium, fourth dome. Mosaic

Venetian disciples) that he attributed the San Marco mosaics.[11] But even within a recension such as that of the Greek Octateuchs, whose geographic affiliations are more purely Byzantine, there were marked developments over the centuries.[12] The fact is that the close tie between a thirteenth-century and a fifth–sixth-century cycle that Tikkanen discovered is far more exceptional than he thought.

This casts doubt not only on the idea of a series of copies mediating between the two monuments but also on Tikkanen's first-named assumption, i.e., that the

Influences" (see note 3 above). However, in the case of one of the manuscripts concerned —the Aelfric Paraphrase of the Pentateuch and Joshua—C. R. Dodwell has recently argued that the illustrations were done straight from the text and that their connections with any traditional cycles are minimal ("L'originalité iconographique de plusieurs illustrations anglo-saxonnes de l'Ancien Testament," *Cahiers de civilisation médiévale* 14 [1971], pp. 319ff.).

11. Tikkanen, *Genesismosaiken*, pp. 87ff., 151ff.

12. K. Weitzmann, "The Octateuch of the Seraglio and the History of its Picture Recension," *Actes du X congrès international d'études byzantines, Istanbul, 15–21 septembre 1955* (Istanbul, 1957), pp. 183ff.

Cotton Bible itself was not the manuscript that served as model for the mosaicists. For my part, I subscribe to the thesis that it probably was. A detailed discussion of this interesting and difficult question would lead us too far afield.[13] The principal stumbling block is the tradition, recorded in the early seventeenth century, that the Cotton manuscript was a present to King Henry VIII from two Greek bishops who brought it from Philippi.[14] But assuming that the tradition is reliable

---

13. See Demus, *Mosaiken*, p. 53; Weitzmann, "Observations," p. 122; idem, "Mosaics of San Marco," p. 152; G. Bonner, "The Cotton Genesis," *British Museum Quarterly* 26 (1962–63), pp. 22ff., especially p. 24f.; H. Buchthal, *Historia Troiana* (London and Leiden, 1971), p. 53f. In the discussion of this problem, undue importance has been attached to the fact that the scene of the Sacrifice of Isaac apparently was already missing from the Cotton Bible when the manuscript was collated in 1703 and is missing also in the San Marco mosaic cycle. Let it be assumed—so the argument goes—that the relevant illustration had been removed from the Cotton manuscript before the thirteenth century; this would explain the absence of this scene from the San Marco mosaics and we could be practically certain that it was this very manuscript that served as their model. But even if the miniature was missing from the codex from which the designs for the mosaics were taken, it is hard to believe that the mosaicists could not, had they so wished, have contrived a representation of this important and frequently depicted event, perhaps with the help of a model from some other source. The principal weakness of the argument, however, lies elsewhere. What is missing at San Marco is not merely this one scene but the entire sequence of events between the Birth and Circumcision of Isaac (Gen. 21:1–7), represented in the western lunette of the second bay, and the beginning of the story of Joseph (Gen. 37) in the dome of the third bay. Illustrations of many of the intervening events—which, be it noted, include the entire story of Jacob—must certainly have been available in the Cotton manuscript. Yet the mosaicists did not devote to these episodes at least one of the spaces that could (and should) have been used to accommodate them. No significance should be attached to the fact that figures of stylite saints were placed in the soffit of the arch separating the second and the third bay. The soffit is narrower than those of the preceding arches (which bear scenes pertaining to Noah and to the Tower of Babel) and thus not well suited for narrative representations. Indeed, none of the ensuing arches was used for scenes, all of them being of the same narrow proportions. What is important, however, is that no Bibilical scenes were placed in the western lunette of the third bay. In this space, which Demus erroneously described as being devoid of mosaic (*Mosaiken*, p. 54), the thirteenth-century mosaicists placed, on either side of a window, two decorative compositions made up of trees, birds, and a fountain. Some circumstance other than an accidental lack of a single illumination must have caused an interruption of the narrative after work on the mosaics in the second bay was completed, and must have prompted the insertion of filler motifs between the Abraham scenes in that bay and the beginning of the Joseph story at the easternmost point of the third dome. Thus the dependence of the mosaics on the Cotton manuscript itself—while, in my opinion, extremely likely—cannot be demonstrated through the missing Sacrifice scene.

14. T. Smith, *Catalogus Librorum Manuscriptorum Bibliothecae Cottonianae* (Oxford, 1696), p. 70f., citing a note of Dr. Richard James, the librarian of Sir Robert Cotton.

—and there is a time lag of more than half a century between the alleged event and the written notice relating to it—it is not, after all, inconceivable that a manuscript that was in northern Greece in the sixteenth century had been in Venice in the thirteenth. The only viable alternative—and a less likely one in my opinion—is that Venice in the Middle Ages possessed what must have been practically a twin to the Cotton Genesis.[15]

Whether the San Marco mosaicists had access to the Cotton Bible itself or to a twin manuscript, the important point is that the appearance in these mosaics of that particular rendering of Genesis stories is not the result of an arrested iconographic development (which is what Tikkanen thought) but rather the use of an actual model of early date. The suggestion has been made that the manuscript had come to Venice only very shortly before work on the mosaics began, as part of the booty from the Fourth Crusade.[16] The fact that there are so many reflections of this particular Genesis iconography in Western art during earlier centuries—and a dearth of such reflections in the Greek East—rather favors the assumption that the manuscript had been in the Latin West for a long time and had spawned at least some of the successive variants of the recension to which I referred earlier.[17] Leap-frogging, as it were, backwards over this Western development, the mosaicists of San Marco—or, more probably, their patrons and advisers—chose for display in the entrance hall of their "Apostoleion" the imagery of a Bible hoary with age (it is interesting to note that the Greeks who brought the Cotton manuscript to Henry VIII allegedly claimed that it had belonged to Origen);[18] and, particularly in the early stages of the work, that imagery was reproduced with quite extraordinary fidelity. It was Otto Demus who put this exercise in antiquarianism in context and elucidated its background.[19] The parallel he drew with what transpired during the same period in the ateliers of the sculptors who worked for San Marco is indeed striking. The imitations of Early Christian marbles that these workshops produced are so faithful that to this day serious scholars are in disagreement as to whether certain pieces are of the fifth century or of the thirteenth. Demus plausibly related this trend to the Venetian's quest for pedigree and authenticity. Recent studies by Hugo Buchthal[20] have thrown further light on

Cf. E. Maunde Thompson, *Catalogue of Ancient Manuscripts in the British Museum*, vol. 1 (London, 1881), p. 20.

15. Cf. Demus, *Mosaiken*, p. 55. Bettini's suggestion (in *Arte Veneta* 21 [1967], p. 24f.) that the mosaicists had before them an "Umbro-Roman" twelfth-century Bible that embodied the iconography of the Cotton Genesis is not convincing.

16. Demus, *Mosaiken*, p. 53.

17. See note 10 above.

18. Smith, *Catalogus*, p. 71.

19. O. Demus, "A Renascence of Early Christian Art in Thirteenth Century Venice," *Late Classical and Mediaeval Studies* (see note 3 above), pp. 348ff.

20. Buchthal, *Historia Troiana*, pp. 54ff.

this phenomenon, which reached a peak in the period following the Fourth Crusade when the first of the Genesis mosaics were made.

Given these rather special circumstances, we should not assume that the San Marco mosaics provide us with an altogether typical example of a relationship between book illumination and monumental painting. In what way this case is, in fact, exceptional will, I hope, become clear as our discussion proceeds.

Let us stay with San Marco a moment longer and ask how, in a purely technical sense, we are to visualize the transfer of images from book to wall. I do not think that the Cotton Genesis (or its twin) can have been continually and routinely accessible to the mosaic workshop. The Cotton Bible was a luxury volume of great value and the same would be true of any twin manuscript. We have just seen that its venerable age was a factor in its being chosen as a model. It seems unlikely that the manuscript itself was made available to the mosaicists for any length of time. If it had been, it would have been in tatters long before the task was finished (let it be remembered that work on the five Genesis bays was protracted over decades).[21] It is a reasonable assumption that sketches or tracings were made from the miniatures to guide the artists in their work.

In this connection it is interesting to cite another mural decoration that provides a close parallel to the Cotton-San Marco relationship. I refer to the frescoes of the late eleventh century in the Church of Saint Julien at Tours, depicting once again scenes from the Old Testament (fig. 6). These, too, have been shown to be copies of miniatures in a codex of venerable age, namely, the so-called Ashburnham Pentateuch (fig. 7), a book known to have been at Tours since the ninth century.[22] David Wright has made the important observation that the miniatures

21. Demus, *Mosaiken*, pp. 42ff., 62ff. Idem, in *Burlington Magazine* 87 (1945), p. 242. S. Bettini, in *Arte Veneta* 8 (1954), p. 22. P. Toesca and F. Forlati, *Mosaics of St. Mark's* (Greenwich, Conn., 1958), p. 17f.

22. A. Grabar, "Fresques romanes copiées sur les miniatures du Pentateuque de Tours," *Cahiers Archéologiques* 9 (1957), pp. 329ff. The only part to have survived of what must have been an extensive fresco decoration is a fragmentary sequence of scenes from Exodus on the west wall of the church. Grabar's study of these scenes is based on watercolor copies made in the late nineteenth century (our fig. 6; cf. ibid., figs. 1, 3, 5, 7; for the corresponding scenes in the Ashburnham Pentateuch see ibid., figs. 2, 4, 6, 8, 9). Two of the scenes recorded—the Adoration of the Golden Calf and the Execution of the Idolaters (ibid., figs. 3, 5)—have no counterparts in miniatures extant in the manuscript, but it is reasonable to assume that they were on a leaf now missing (ibid., pp. 332ff.). Mrs. A. S. Cahn's attempt (in *Cahiers Archéologiques* 16 [1966], pp. 203ff.) to prove the existence of these scenes in the manuscript by relating to them the traces of a miniature on a stub between the present folios 133 and 134 has been shown to be untenable; see B. Narkiss, in *Cahiers Archéologiques* 22 (1972), pp. 32ff. There is, however, room for the missing miniatures between the present folios 83 and 84 (ibid., p. 38). Even so, some rearrangement of the sequence of subjects in the miniatures on the part of the designer of the Saint Julien frescoes must be reckoned with. For the two scenes in question were placed by him between two subjects derived respectively from the

display signs of tracings having been made from them; and it is tempting to assume—though, of course, not provable—that these tracings were made in conjunction with the work on the frescoes of Saint Julien.[23] Perhaps if the Cotton Genesis were in better condition similar observations could be made on its miniatures (always assuming that it and not a twin manuscript was in Venice). In any case, it should be noticed that in one respect, that of color, the San Marco mosaics have been found not to agree at all with the illustrations in the Cotton Bible.[24] If, as I suggest, the immediate model of the mosaics was a set of outline drawings made from the codex, such a disagreement would not be surprising.

I assume then at San Marco an intermediate link between illuminated book and mosaic—not a *Zwischenglied* in the sense postulated by Tikkanen (i.e., another Bible), but a set of working drawings. Such essentially utilitarian drawings or paintings must have been in wide use by medieval muralists. I have discussed some of the evidence for these so-called pictorial guides on other occasions,[25] but must return to the subject briefly in the present context. For I believe that pictorial guides were a common link between the work of the illuminator and that of the mosaicist or fresco painter.

Undoubtedly there were other instances aside from the vestibule mosaics at San Marco and the frescoes at Saint Julien at Tours where a monumental decoration was based on a library book. Though every codex used in this manner need not have been—and probably was not—as old and venerable as the Cotton Genesis, I think in such cases one should normally reckon with drawings or sketches as intermediaries. What I have said in regard to the Cotton manuscript surely applies to a greater or lesser degree to library codices generally (and, of course, to illuminated service books as well): they were too valuable to be left in a muralist's atelier, to say nothing of being used on a scaffold. By the same token, however, pictorial guides must have been considered expendable and must have been subject to a very high rate of attrition. It is not surprising, therefore, that their existence is often a matter of inference rather than direct evidence.

We know a little more about pictorial guides for mural decorations derived from other mural decorations than we do about those based on library books. As early as A.D. 403, Paulinus of Nola and his friend Sulpicius Severus, busy building churches in southern Italy and in Gaul, respectively, exchanged not only *tituli* and

---

upper and lower register of one and the same miniature (fol. 76; cf. Grabar, op. cit., figs. 1, 3, 4, 5, 7, 9). A further study of this problem has been promised by Professor Narkiss (op. cit., p. 38).

23. D. H. Wright, in *Art Bulletin* 43 (1961), p. 250.

24. Tikkanen, *Genesismosaiken*, p. 114. Demus, *Mosaiken*, p. 56.

25. Kitzinger, *Mosaics of Monreale*, pp. 43ff., 62f. Idem in *Byzantine Art. An European Art: Lectures* (Athens, 1966), p. 140. Idem, in *Art Bulletin* 50 (1968), p. 291 (review of V. Lazarev, *Old Russian Murals and Mosaics*).

Fig. 6. Scenes from Exodus (copy by Yperman). Tours, Saint Julien. Frescoes

verse inscriptions accompanying the pictorial decorations of their churches but also the *picturae* themselves. In sending his friend this documentation from two churches at Nola and Fundi, Paulinus wrote expressly that Sulpicius might wish to choose one of them as a model for the decoration of a church he was then building.[26]

One set of drawings recording a monumental picture cycle for use in producing a new one is actually known, though it belongs to a much later period. A well-known rotulus of the early thirteenth century in the Cathedral Library of Vercelli displays in the form of outline drawings a long series of scenes from the Book of Acts copied from paintings in the Church of Saint Eusebius (fig. 8).[27]

26. Paulinus of Nola, Epist. 32, ch. 9, 10, 17 (ed. W. v. Hartel, Corpus scriptorum ecclesiasticorum latinorum, vol. 29 [Vienna, Prague, and Leipzig, 1894], pp. 285, 291; for an English translation of chapter 17—not entirely accurate in the crucial passage—see R. C. Goldschmidt, *Paulinus' Churches at Nola* [Amsterdam, 1940], pp. 45ff.; cf. also C. Davis-Weyer, *Early Medieval Art 300–1150*, Sources and Documents in the History of Art Series [Englewood Cliffs, N.J., 1971], p. 23). It is interesting to note that the church at Fundi was not yet finished when Paulinus sent his friend the *pictura* destined for its apse. In all probability, therefore, what Paulinus sent was a copy of a preparatory design. For the date of the letter see Goldschmidt, op. cit., p. 17.

27. C. Cipolla, "La pergamena rappresentante le antiche pitture della Basilica di S. Eusebio in Vercelli," *R. Deputazione sovra gli studi di storia patria per le antiche provincie e la Lombardia: Miscellanea di storia italiana*, series 3, vol. 6 (1901), pp. 1ff. R. W. Scheller, *A Survey of Medieval Model Books* (Haarlem, 1963), pp. 94ff.

Fig. 7. Scenes from Exodus. Paris, Bibliothèque Nationale, cod. n. a. lat. 2334 (Ashburnham Pentateuch), fol. 76

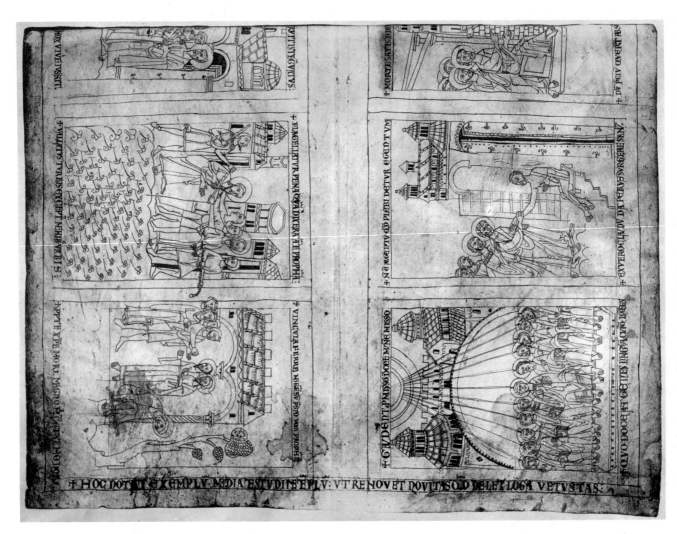

Fig. 8. Rotulus reproducing scenes from Acts in Church of Saint Eusebius (detail). Vercelli, Archivio Capitolare (after Cipolla)

In the accompanying verses it is explained that these copies were to serve as *exempla* in a restoration.[28] The Vercelli Rotulus thus can give us an idea of what pictorial guides looked like. In this instance the two decorations involved happened to have been in the same building. But similar records may be assumed to have served as intermediaries in cases of close and specific resemblances between murals in different places.[29] To quote one such instance with which I have long been concerned, the relationship that exists between certain parts of the decoration in the Cappella Palatina in Palermo of ca. 1140–60, on the one hand, and in the Cathedral of Monreale of ca. 1180–90, on the other, in my opinion requires the assumption that drawings were made of mosaics in the former church for use in designing those of the latter.[30] Specific agreements, particularly between the Old Testament cycles and the cycles from the lives of Saints Peter and Paul (figs. 9–12) in the two churches, cannot be explained adequately by assuming that both are based on the same miniature models or (as has been thought) on related miniature models stemming from the same school. There must have been drawings that conveyed the iconography of the Cappella Palatina cycle itself to the artists at Monreale, and we may imagine these drawings to have been somewhat like those in the Vercelli Roll. This, however, also means that the Monreale artists exercised considerable freedom vis-à-vis these *exempla*. Iconographic elements were added from other sources as well (and, at least in the case of the Old Testament cycle, there is reason to believe that one of these additional sources may have been the pictorial guide on which the Cappella Palatina mosaics had in turn been based and which may have been still available). Compositions were changed not only to adapt them to differently shaped spaces but also to conform with new aesthetic requirements. Above all, there was a total stylistic transformation (figs. 11 and 12). Thus the later cycles were, in effect, new creations. But these cycles in turn were available for copying with a view to use elsewhere. We have, in fact, miniature copies made from mosaics at Monreale in the late thirteenth century, though these copies served as text illustrations.[31]

28. Cipolla, "La pergamena," pp. 7ff. Scheller, *Survey*, p. 95. Cf. R. Oertel, "Wandmalerei und Zeichnung in Italien," *Mitteilungen des Kunsthistorischen Institutes in Florenz* 5 (1937–40), pp. 217ff., especially p. 231.

29. Oertel, "Wandmalerei," pp. 230ff. L. Tintori and M. Meiss, *The Painting of the Life of St. Francis in Assisi* (New York, 1962), p. 34.

30. For this and what follows, see Kitzinger, *Mosaics of Monreale*, pp. 33ff.

31. H. Buchthal, "Some Sicilian Miniatures of the Thirteenth Century," *Miscellanea pro arte: Festschrift für Hermann Schnitzler* (Düsseldorf, 1965), pp. 185ff.; see also W. C. Loerke, "The Monumental Miniature," in the present volume. Miniatures were based on mosaics in the Cappella Palatina as well; see H. Buchthal, "Notes on a Sicilian Manuscript of the Early Fourteenth Century," *Essays in the History of Art Presented to Rudolf Wittkower* (London, 1967), pp. 36ff., and Loerke, "The Monumental Miniature."

HIC CONVERS PAVLF BAPTISAT · AB ANANIA ·

HIC DISPVTANDO PAVLVS COFVDIT IVDEOS

SCS PAVLV

PAVLVS P̄ FENESTRAM IN SPORTA DIMISSVS · PERICVLV EFFVGIT IN DAMASCENO · VRB

PAVLVS TRADIT EPISTOLAS DISCIPVLIS SVI TIMOTHEO ET SILBE DE TERRA PAVLVS VORBE

S· PAVLVS

Fig. 9. Scenes from Life of Saint Paul. Monreale, Cathedral. Mosaic

Fig. 10. Saint Paul's Disputation at Damascus and Flight. Palermo, Cappella Palatina. Mosaic

In addition to pictorial guides prepared *ad hoc* for the execution of some one specific mural decoration,[32] there were also what may be called generic guides,

32. I have discussed here only instances involving known monumental decorations. There are, aside from the Vercelli Rotulus, other Western miniature cycles that on the strength of internal evidence may be claimed to have been intended as pictorial guides for specific large-scale decorations, though the precise nature and location of these decorations elude us; see Scheller, *Survey*, pp. 97ff. (Paris, Bib. Nat. ms. lat. 11907, fols. 231ff.); R. Branner, "Le Rouleau de saint Éloi," *L'information de l'histoire de l'art* 12 (1967), pp. 55ff.; idem, "The Saint-Quentin Rotulus," *Scriptorium* 21 (1967), pp. 252ff.

Ernst Kitzinger

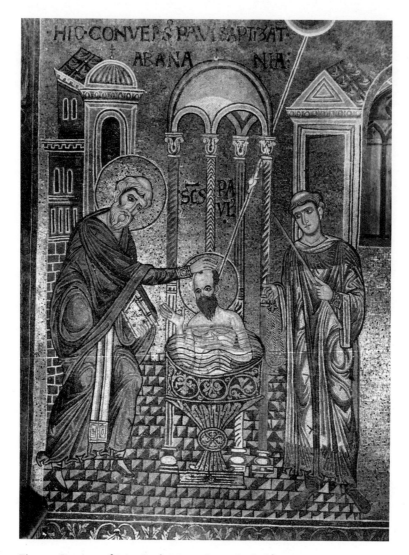

Fig. 11. Baptism of Saint Paul. Monreale, Cathedral. Mosaic

pictorial manuals designed from the outset for repeated use and thus comparable to the *podlinniks* of post-medieval Russia. In the present context these generic guides are of particular interest, though the evidence for them is, if anything, even scantier.

No actual example of such a book incontrovertibly intended for use in mural decoration is known.[33] We do, however, have pertinent references in literary

33. An extensive, though unfinished and fragmentary series of Old and New Testament scenes in Berlin (Kupferstichkabinett, ms. 78A6), executed in the Meuse region in the second half of the twelfth century and not associated with any text other

Fig. 12. Baptism of Saint Paul. Palermo, Cappella Palatina. Mosaic

sources. The most important of these references are in a hagiographic text of
the eighth century not yet adequately published and studied, namely, the Life
of Saint Pancratius of Tauromenium. Written in southern Italy in a Greek milieu,

than brief captions, has sometimes been considered a model book for goldsmiths or
other artists, partly because of an indubitable relationship to the scenes on the font of
Rainer of Huy at Liège (ca. A.D. 1110) and other metalwork in the area (H. Swarzenski,
Monuments of Romanesque Art, 2d ed. [London, 1967], pp. 31, 58 and pls. 112f., 167;
Scheller, *Survey*, pp. 69ff. *Rhein und Maas* [exhibition catalogue, Cologne, 1972], p.
296f.). A full study of this important book and the single leaves related to it is being prepared by Dr. Swarzenski.

in which there was opposition to Byzantine Iconoclasm, this apocryphal account of the missionary activities of Saint Peter and the Christianization of Sicily is copiously interlarded with references to religious images.[34] Though the action is laid in the first century A.D., these references may be assumed to reflect practices of the author's own time. Saint Peter sees to it that all newly built churches in the entire area between Jerusalem and Antioch receive painted decorations; and he instructs Pancratius, the disciple he sends as a missionary to Sicily, to do the same there. For this purpose he has a painter execute models under his own instructions. Referred to variously as volumes, panels, folding panels, and papyri,[35] these picture cycles, which comprised the whole story of the Life of Christ from the Annunciation to the Ascension, clearly were made expressly as prototypes for wall decorations. Along with patens and chalices and copies of the Gospels and Epistles, they figure among the equipment with which the missionary is provided to set up churches in his territory. To the writer the idea of a standard decoration laid down once and for all in canonical form (and indeed, in this case, by no less an authority than Saint Peter himself) evidently is a familiar and natural one.

Perhaps I should also cite in this context the famous description by the Venerable Bede of how Benedict Biscop in the late seventh century went about building and furnishing the churches of his newly founded Northumbrian monasteries of Wearmouth and Jarrow. Among the treasures that Benedict brought back from his several journeys to Rome were paintings (referred to by Bede as *imagines* or *picturae* or *picturae imaginum*) of the Virgin Mary and the Apostles, the Gospel story, the Book of Revelation, and Old and New Testament scenes in typological confrontation.[36] Intended for the adornment of the walls of the newly built churches, these may well have been small-scale prototypes of the kind referred to, not more than a century later, in the Life of Saint Pancratius. However, the

34. See the extracts published by A. N. Veselovskii (*Iz istorii romana i povesti*, Sbornik otdielenia russkago iazyka i slovesnosti imperatorskoi akademii nauk, vol. 40, no. 2 [Saint Petersburg, 1886], p. 75f.) and H. Usener (*Kleine Schriften*, vol. 4 [Leipzig and Berlin, 1913], p. 417f.); cf. C. Mango, *The Art of the Byzantine Empire 312–1453*, Sources and Documents in the History of Art Series (Englewood Cliffs, N.J., 1972), p. 137f. For the date of the text see E. Patlagean, "Les Moines grecs d'Italie et l'apologie des thèses pontificales (VIIIᵉ–IXᵉ siècles)," *Studi Medievali*, series 3, vol. 5 (1964), pp. 579ff., especially pp. 587ff. (I owe this reference to Ihor Ševčenko).

35. ... τόμους δύο τῶν θείων ἱστοριῶν ἔχοντας τὴν διακόσμησιν τῆς ἐκκλησίας ἤγουν τὴν εἰκονικὴν ἱστορίαν τῆς παλαιᾶς τε καὶ νέας διαθήκης ... καὶ λαβὼν τοὺς πίνακας ... καὶ ἀναπτύξας ... (Veselovskii, op. cit., p. 75f.); ἐνετυποῦσαν αὐτὰς ἐν πίναξιν ἢ χαρτώοις ... (Usener, op. cit., p. 418). For χαρτῷος see G. W. H. Lampe, *A Patristic Greek Lexicon* (Oxford, 1961), p. 1520.

36. Bede, Lives of the Abbots, chapters 7 and 9 (*Baedae opera historica*, vol. 2, ed. J. E. King, Loeb Classical Library [London and New York, 1930], pp. 404, 412ff.). Cf. Davis-Weyer (see note 26 above), p. 74f.

Fig. 13. Christ on Lake Tiberias. Florence, Museo Archeologico. Papyrus fragment (after Minto)

possibility cannot be excluded that they were full-sized paintings on wood or canvas that were bodily affixed to the walls.

Be this as it may, generic pictorial guides undoubtedly did exist. As a possible exiguous scrap from such a guide, I cite a papyrus fragment in the Museo Archeologico in Florence, perhaps of the fifth century, showing in outline drawing the scene of the Storm on the Sea of Galilee, with Christ asleep in the boat in the company of his disciples (fig. 13). This, of course, could also be a drawing made *ad hoc* in preparation of some particular painting. In any case, however, it is not a text illustration (on the back is a rent document).[37] I also want to draw attention to a set of drawings of a much later period and from a different region, a sixteenth-century Armenian manuscript in Venice published, or rather republished, a few years ago by Sirarpie Der Nersessian. This was certainly a generic guide, a pictorial counterpart to the famous Mount Athos manual, as Miss Der Nersessian says. In this case, however, internal evidence of the manuscript points to the drawings being intended for use by miniaturists, while in part their sources, according to Miss der Nersessian, were monumental paintings.[38] In other words,

37. A. Minto, in *Bollettino d'arte*, series 2, vol. 5 (1925–26), p. 190 and fig. 3f. G. Bovini, *Monumenti figurati paleocristiani conservati a Firenze*, Monumenti di antichità cristiana, series 2, vol. 6 (Vatican City, 1950), p. 51f.

38. S. Der Nersessian, "Copies de peintures byzantines dans un carnet arménien de 'modeles,'" *Cahiers Archéologiques* 18 (1968), pp. 111ff. The manuscript consists of two parts. The drawings derived from monumental paintings are in the second part. For the first part, see eadem, "Le carnet de modeles d'un miniaturiste arménien," *Armeniaca: Mélanges d'études arméniennes* (Venice, 1969), pp. 175ff.

this example once again would seem to document the process of transmission from wall to book. But generic guides surely were a natural—and perhaps the most normal—link in the opposite direction as well.

Indeed, it stands to reason that such guides for muralists—the volumes, panels, and papyri referred to in the Life of Saint Pancratius—often were the work of ateliers and artists engaged in the illustration of texts. And thus pictures and cycles originally invented for this latter purpose would naturally find their way into mural contexts. To use Kurt Weitzmann's term, they would "migrate."[39] It may well have been in the ateliers producing pictorial guides, more than anywhere else, that the relationship between text illustration and wall decoration had its *Sitz im Leben*. But, as we have seen, in this transfer of patterns, wall decoration was not always and necessarily at the receiving end.[40] Each case must be judged on its own merits. We must also reckon with the possibility that a miniaturist, when preparing a pictorial guide, refashioned or rearranged his material with a view to its use in a monumental context. To give just one example: if the typological series of Old Testament and New Testament scenes brought to Northumbria by Benedict Biscop was indeed a pictorial guide rather than a set of large-scale paintings, the scenes must already have been paired off with a view to their antithetic display on the walls of a church.[41]

Another and more difficult question is whether or to what extent the muralist's stylistic rendering of his subjects was predetermined by these pictorial guides. Obviously this depends in part on how elaborate they were. Often they may only have provided essential iconographic schemes in outline form,[42] leaving it to the executant artist to work out the detail in terms of scale, architectural context, and his own stylistic training and preferences.

Here I must return once more to the San Marco Genesis cycle. In this instance the drawings that I presume to have been the link between miniatures and mosaics must have faithfully preserved not only the iconography but also much of the style of the former. For, as we have seen, the mosaics, at least in the first bays, reflect that style. But this may be another respect in which these mosaics are not quite the typical case Tikkanen thought them to be. It should be borne in mind that in Tikkanen's day medieval mosaics were widely thought to have been executed with the help of full-scale cartoons,[43] which, indeed, might be more or

39. K. Weitzmann, *Illustrations in Roll and Codex* (Princeton, 1947; second printing, with addenda, 1970), passim.

40. See notes 31 and 38 above, and W. C. Loerke's essay in the present volume.

41. See note 36 above.

42. See figs. 8 and 13; Der Nersessian, "Copies de peintures," figs. 1–9.

43. Thus G. Millet, relying on information furnished him by the Venetian restorer Novo, thought that the mosaics of Daphni were produced by the *al rovescio* method, i.e., with the help of full-sized, fully colored cartoons or canvases to which the tesserae

less mechanical enlargements of miniatures. With this as a premise, the use of illuminations such as those of the Cotton Genesis would be nothing out of the ordinary. But nineteenth-century thinking in these matters was greatly influenced by the practices in contemporary mosaic ateliers, which normally did base their work on fully elaborated paintings.[44] Today we know that such cartoons came into use only in the fifteenth century, when the medieval craft tradition of mosaic-making had broken down.[45] All the investigations of recent decades indicate that the medieval mosaicist's work was to a large extent a freehand operation.[46] There was no room in his procedure for a full-scale cartoon, and hence no room for a process of mechanical enlargement from miniature models. Miniatures were not projected on the wall in the manner of lantern slides, so to speak. Rather did they serve as a guide to the muralist in drawing up his compositions on the surface itself. For this purpose fairly sketchy outline drawings would normally be sufficient. And even in the rather special case of the San Marco Genesis cycle, we found that the authority of the miniature model in matters of style was not absolute. The mosaicists exercised some freedom from the outset, and their independence increased as work progressed.[47] An example such as the Peter and Paul cycle of Monreale, where an iconography prescribed by a particular guide was reproduced throughout in terms of the executant artists' own repertory of stylistic forms (figs. 9 and 11), may be a good deal more typical.

The foregoing remarks raise broad and general questions concerning the influence upon monumental painting of styles characteristic of or first introduced in

---

were affixed in the studio before being placed on the wall (*Le Monastère de Daphni* [Paris, 1899], p. 165f.) See also the chapter on technique in Gerspach's *La Mosaique* (Paris, n.d. [1881], pp. 235ff.), where the use of (evidently full-sized) models and a mechanical *décalquage* of such models onto the mosaicist's working surface are taken for granted (cf. especially pp. 236, 243f.).

44. G. Bovini, in *Enciclopedia Universale dell'Arte*, vol. 9 (Venice and Rome, 1963), col. 701.

45. Ibid., col. 700. Cf. M. Muraro, "The Statutes of the Venetian *Arti* and the Mosaics of the Mascoli Chapel," *Art Bulletin* 43 (1961), pp. 263ff. For the decline of the medieval craft tradition in mosaic work, see A. Chastel, "La Mosaique à Venise et à Florence au XVᵉ siècle," *Arte Veneta* 8 (1954), pp. 119ff.; and for the coming into use of cartoons in fifteenth-century mural decoration generally, Oertel, "Wandmalerei" (see note 28 above), pp. 222, 312f.; Tintori and Meiss, *St. Francis*, (see note 29 above) pp. 13, 17ff.

46. See Kitzinger, *Mosaics of Monreale*, pp. 64ff., with further references. Idem, in *Enciclopedia Universale dell'Arte*, vol. 9 (Venice and Rome, 1963), col. 674. P. A. Underwood, *The Kariye Djami*, vol 1 (New York, 1966), pp. 172ff., especially p. 177f.

47. See above, p. 102 and figs. 1, 3, and 5. Comparing the finished mosaic with the outline drawing discovered by F. Forlati on the first rendering coat under one of the

miniatures. In the present context I cannot deal with this problem in comprehensive fashion. But I shall devote the final section of this paper to one particular mural decoration whose relationship to book illumination I believe to be primarily and emphatically visual and stylistic.

The monument in question is the series of fifth-century mosaic panels with scenes from the Old Testament on the nave walls of Santa Maria Maggiore in Rome.[48] Like the Genesis scenes in San Marco, they display a close relationship with miniatures. But unlike the San Marco cycle, that of Santa Maria Maggiore has proved singularly unamenable to attempts to relate it to any of the known recensions of Biblical illustration. This is the problem on which I want to comment. It will be my contention that the Santa Maria Maggiore mosaics, while visually (and purposefully) evocative of pictures in books, are not actually derived from an illustrated codex.

Originally there were on each side of the nave twenty-one panels. The stories depicted pertained respectively to Abraham and Jacob and to Moses and Joshua. Of the total of forty-two panels, twenty-seven have survived wholly or at least in part. Many of these panels illustrate sequentially successive events in the lives of the four heroes. Sometimes an entire panel is given over to a single scene. More often two scenes are superimposed in registers.

Three illuminated manuscripts are customarily adduced for comparison with these mosaics: the Quedlinburg Itala;[49] the Vatican Vergil;[50] and the *Iliad* in the Ambrosian Library in Milan.[51] None of these manuscripts is securely dated—indeed, their dating has been based in part on comparisons with Santa Maria Maggiore—but all certainly belong to the same general period. The most distant, as far as place (and date?) of manufacture is concerned, is probably the Milan *Iliad*.[52]

---

scenes in the first bay, one can see that the muralists introduced changes not only vis-à-vis their miniature model but also vis-à-vis their own preliminary sketches on the wall itself (see *Arte Veneta* 3 [1949], pp. 85ff. and figs. 82ff.).

48. C. Cecchelli, *I mosaici della Basilica di S. Maria Maggiore* (Turin, 1956), pp. 105ff. and pls. 14–46. H. Karpp, *Die frühchristlichen und mittelalterlichen Mosaiken in Santa Maria Maggiore zu Rom* (Baden-Baden, 1966), pls. 29–157.

49. Berlin, Staatsbibliothek, ms. theol. lat. fol. 485 (H. Degering and A. Boeckler, *Die Quedlinburger Italafragmente* [Berlin, 1932]).

50. Ms. Vat. lat. 3225 (J. de Wit, *Die Miniaturen des Vergilius Vaticanus* [Amsterdam, 1959]).

51. Ms. F. 205 P. Inf. (*Ilias Ambrosiana*, Fontes Ambrosiani, vol. 28 [Bern and Olten, 1953]. R. Bianchi Bandinelli, *Hellenistic-Byzantine Miniatures of the Iliad* [Olten, 1955]).

52. Bianchi Bandinelli came to the conclusion that the manuscript was executed in Constantinople in the first years of the sixth century (*Hellenistic-Byzantine Miniatures*, p. 165). Weitzmann prefers an attribution to Alexandria and a date in the fifth century (see his review in *Gnomon* 29 [1957], pp. 606ff., especially p. 615f.).

Since none of these codices has the same subject content as the Santa Maria Maggiore mosaics, the relationship here can only be formal and stylistic. That relationship, however, is unmistakable (figs. 14ff.).[53] It is true that it extends only to certain parts of the mosaic cycle. It is true also that in none of the three codices are there miniatures whose formal makeup is comparable to that of the mosaics in *all* respects.[54] Certain compositions, however, are remarkably similar in the relationship of figures, buildings, and frames (cf. figs. 14 and 17; 15 and 18). The types used for buildings and figures also tend to be similar, and there is the same lack of consistency in their respective scale. The ground on which they are placed recedes into a hazy distance; and mosaicists as well as miniaturists suggest this openness of space by a succession of horizontal zones of different hues often softly and subtly merging one into the other. In the miniatures, the horizontal layering of these atmospheric settings is more schematic than it is in many of the mosaics. But the undulating skylines that often appear in the latter (fig. 18) can be found in the former also (fig. 16).[55] So can the bird's-eye view with a distant diagonal shoreline, which the mosaicist used to accommodate the masses of figures he needed to depict the Crossing of the Red Sea (fig. 20; cf. fig. 19). The panel is one of the few that are given over to a single scene. The superimposition of two scenes in a single square frame that so many of the mosaics show occurs repeatedly in the Milan *Iliad* (fig. 21).[56] As for the frames themselves, they also resemble those used by the miniaturists.[57]

There is no need to continue further with detailed comparisons, the less so since these relationships are well known. Also, for our purpose the specific detail counts for less than the overall resemblances between mosaics and miniatures. In

53. Cf. Boeckler, in Degering and Boeckler, *Italafragmente*, pp. 182ff.; De Wit, *Vergilius Vaticanus*, p. 155; Bianchi Bandinelli, *Hellenistic-Byzantine Miniatures*, pp. 146ff. and passim (see index, s.v. "Rome, Sta. Maria Maggiore").

54. Koehler, *Die Schule von Tours*, part 2 (see note 10 above), p. 172f., laid stress on differences between style elements in the mosaics of Santa Maria Maggiore, on the one hand, and the miniatures in the Itala and Vergil manuscripts, on the other.

55. Degering and Boeckler, *Italafragmente*, pl. 4 (pictures 7 and 8); cf. e.g., Karpp, *Mosaiken*, pls. 125, 128, 133, 138, 153.

56. *Iliad*, pictures VI–VII; XVI–XVII; XX–XXI; XXXI–XXXII; XLIV–XLV; XLIX–L (our fig. 21); see Bianchi Bandinelli, *Hellenistic-Byzantine Miniatures*, pp. 13, 133ff. For two-register panels as a convention in miniature painting see Weitzmann, in *Gnomon* 29 (1957), p. 613f. But see also p. 134, below, and note 73.

57. See for instance Karpp, *Mosaiken*, figs. 118 and 128 (our figs. 17 and 18), where the original frame appears to be preserved at the top of the panel. For this type of frame—with an outer red and an inner dark band separated by a white line—compare the Vatican Vergil (De Wit, *Vergilius Vaticanus*, p. 175). The frames of the *Iliad* miniatures are also similar, though they lack the white line (Bianchi Bandinelli, *Hellenistic-Byzantine Miniatures*, p. 92).

124

Fig. 16. Illustrations to I Samuel 15. Berlin, Staatsbibliothek, cod. theol. lat. fol. 485 (Quedlinburg Itala)

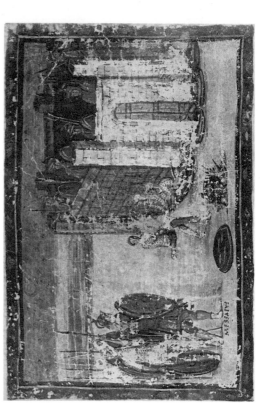

Fig. 14. Rome, Vatican Library, cod. lat. 3225 (Vergil), fol. 33v

Fig. 15. Rome, Vatican Library, cod. lat. 3225 (Vergil), fol. 72v

125

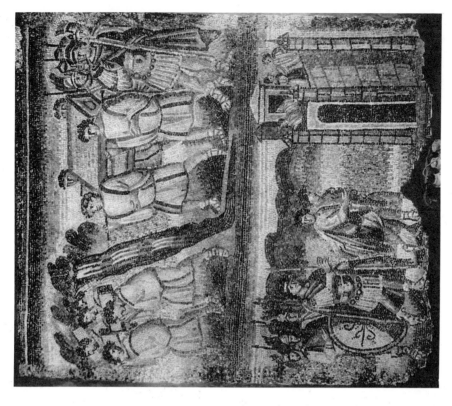

Fig. 18. Joshua scenes. Rome, Santa Maria Maggiore. Mosaic

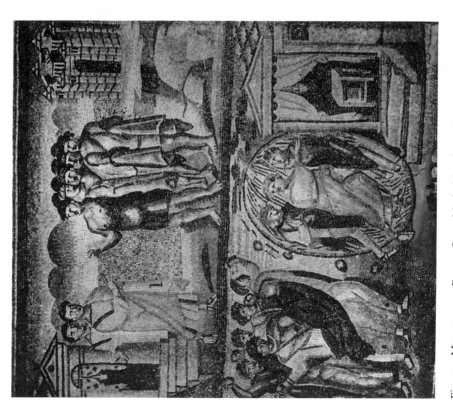

Fig. 17. Moses scenes. Rome, Santa Maria Maggiore. Mosaic

Fig. 19. Milan, Biblioteca Ambrosiana, cod. F. 205 P. Inf. (*Iliad*), fol. 7v

my opinion there can be no doubt that to a fifth-century beholder mosaic panels such as those in figs. 17 and 18 must have conjured up visual associations with illuminated books with which he was familiar. I am aware of a potential fallacy here: framed miniatures of the kind we find in our three codices, with figures in landscapes and atmospheric settings, perpetuate a tradition that, in turn, was rooted in monumental painting.[58] But this tradition belongs to a much earlier period.[59] Muralists of the fourth and fifth centuries had not maintained it. For a

58. Cf. Bianchi Bandinelli, *Hellenistic-Byzantine Miniatures*, p. 146, n. 2; K. Weitzmann, "Book Illustration of the Fourth Century: Tradition and Innovation," *Akten des VII. Internationalen Kongresses für Christliche Archäologie, Trier, 5.–11. September 1965* (Rome and Berlin, 1969), pp. 257ff., especially p. 260ff. (see idem, *Studies in Classical and Byzantine Manuscript Illumination*, ed. H. L. Kessler [Chicago and London, 1971], pp. 96ff., especially pp. 98ff.).

59. Cf., e.g., panels with mythological scenes on a ceiling in Nero's Domus Aurea (*Enciclopedia dell'arte antica, classica e orientale*, vol. 6 [Rome, 1965], color plate facing p. 960).

127

Fig. 20. Crossing of the Red Sea. Rome, Santa Maria Maggiore. Mosaic

viewer of that period the format, particularly when applied to a sequential series of stories, must have suggested an illustrated codex.

It is all the more strange that it should have proved so difficult to relate the iconography of this cycle to any of the known families of illustrated Old Testament books. For the Joshua scenes, it is true, a number of scholars have claimed a connection with the pictorial tradition that later produced the famous Byzantine rotulus in the Vatican and the Byzantine Octateuchs.[60] But Kurt Weitzmann has pointed out, rightly in my view, that this relationship is of a rather general kind.[61] Yet in the Joshua sequence the "miniature" character of the mosaics is very much in evidence. Here, if anywhere, one should be able to establish the kind of connection that Tikkanen discovered for the Genesis scenes in San Marco.

It is, of course, possible that the Santa Maria Maggiore mosaics are based on a Bible now lost. But there is internal evidence in the mosaics themselves that suggests that they were not created in the manner of the San Marco cycle. It has repeatedly been remarked that, despite a basic uniformity of workmanship, they fall into two distinct stylistic groups. In addition to scenes such as those I have referred to, with impressionist and atmospheric settings and relatively small figures inhabiting these settings, there are others in which large and monumental figures dominate the composition entirely, space and settings are reduced or eliminated, and panels are organized rather in terms of surface patterns created

60. C. R. Morey, *Early Christian Art*, 2d ed. (Princeton, 1953), pp. 146ff. (some of the Moses scenes are here also related to the Octateuch tradition). C.-O. Nordström, "Rabbinica in frühchristlichen und byzantinischen Illustrationen zum 4. Buch Mose," *Figura* (= Uppsala Studies in the History of Art), n.s. 1, 1959, pp. 24ff., especially p. 25. J. Kollwitz, "Der Josuazyklus von S. Maria Maggiore," *Römische Quartalschrift* 61 (1966), pp. 106ff.

61. K. Weitzmann, "Zur Frage des Einflusses jüdischer Bilderquellen auf die Illustration des Alten Testamentes," *Mullus: Festschrift Theodor Klauser* (= *Jahrbuch für Antike und Christentum*, supplement vol. 1 [Münster, 1964]), pp. 401ff., especially p. 411f. (reprinted in, *Studies* [see note 58 above], pp. 76ff., especially p. 90f.). Note must be taken also of the fact that the spear, as distinct from a sword, held by the Captain of the Host of the Lord in his appearance to Joshua (Karpp, *Mosaiken*, fig. 133) corresponds neither to the Septuagint nor to the Vulgate text of Jos. 5:13, but only to the Old Latin version (P. Künzle, "Per una visione organica dei mosaici antichi di S. Maria Maggiore," *Atti della Pontificia Accademia Romana di Archeologia: Rendiconti* 34 [1961–62], pp. 153ff., especially p. 162). G. Henderson has discerned some relationships between the Joshua cycle in Santa Maria Maggiore and that in the Aelfric manuscript in the British Museum ("The Joshua Cycle in B. M. Cotton Ms. Claudius B. IV," *Journal of the British Archaeological Association*, series 3, vol. 31 [1968], pp. 38ff.). But, with the possible exception of the rendering of the two spies escaping from Jericho (ibid., p. 48f. and pl. 4, fig. 1), these relationships again appear to be only of a very general kind. See also note 10 above for Dodwell's thesis that the Aelfric illustrations are essentially based on the text itself.

Fig. 21. Milan, Biblioteca Ambrosiana, cod. F. 205 P. Inf. (*Iliad*), fol. 44v

by the figures.[62] To try to account for this difference by assuming that the two groups belonged to different periods is clearly impossible. Rather must we see the two kinds of mosaics as done in different "modes" or "keys" in the musical sense; that is to say, for certain scenes the artist deliberately adopted a more solemn, more ceremonial manner, a *largo* as against an *allegro* style, to preserve the musical analogy.[63] Now this solemn mode comes to the fore particularly in

62. R. Kömstedt, *Vormittelalterliche Malerei* (Augsburg, 1929), pp. 14ff. Künzle, "Per una visione organica," pp. 158ff. See also M. Schapiro as cited in the next note.

63. On "modes" see M. Schapiro's review of Morey's *Early Christian Art* in *The Review of Religion* 8 (1943–44), pp. 165ff., especially pp. 181ff. (p. 182 for the two "modes" in the Santa Maria Maggiore mosaics); E. Kitzinger, *Byzantine Art in the Period between Justinian and Iconoclasm*, Berichte zum XI. Internationalen Byzantinisten-Kongress, München, 1958, IV, 1 (Munich, 1958), pp. 36f., 47f.; J. Bialostocki, "Das Modusproblem in den bildenden Künsten," *Zeitschrift für Kunstgeschichte* 24 (1961), pp. 128ff.

the panels nearest the sanctuary of the church (e.g., fig. 22). From these it carries over into the New Testament scenes on the triumphal arch, which are done in the latter manner entirely. Some years ago Father Künzle concluded from this observation—correctly, it seems to me—that the Old Testament scenes cannot be straightforward copies from a book. They must have been designed with a view to their location in the building.[64] Nor is this merely a question of the kind of change a muralist might introduce on his own, vis-à-vis a miniature cycle, as his work progressed. I have referred to changes of that kind in the later part of the San Marco Genesis cycle. But there they only concerned incidentals and did not affect the iconographic substance.

Some of these ceremonial scenes do, in fact, have specific sources of inspiration in other categories of Late Antique imagery. Abraham's encounter with Melchizedek calls to mind an imperial *adventus*.[65] The adoption of Moses by Pharaoh's daughter suggests an imperial audience scene.[66] Moses' marriage (fig. 22) is modeled on the *dextrarum junctio* in Roman monumental art. André Grabar has noted the relationship of these scenes to imperial and triumphal representations; and, of course, influences from that source are in evidence even more in the scenes from Christ's infancy on the arch of the sanctuary.[67]

There can be no doubt that this evocation of Roman imperial art was deliberate and meaningful. At a time in which the papacy emerged as the only effective power left in the Eternal City, the imagery of Santa Maria Maggiore proclaimed the *Roma Christiana* as the rightful heir and successor to the Rome of the Caesars. Much has been written on this "Roman" aspect of the church and its decoration, and I need not elaborate on this topic.[68] The point I wish to make is that that part of the Old Testament cycle which is cast in the "impressionist" mode—and this is by far the largest one—is also rooted in the same concept. It too is meant to evoke

64. Künzle, "Per una visione organica," p. 162 (with further references).

65. A. Grabar, *Christian Iconography*, Bollingen Series XXXV-10 (Princeton, 1968), fig. 143f.

66. Ibid., fig. 132.

67. Ibid., pp. 46ff.; for the imperial affinities of the mosaics on the arch, see idem, *L'Empereur dans l'art byzantin* (Paris, 1936), pp. 211ff.; also E. H. Kantorowicz, "Puer Exoriens: On the Hypapante in the Mosaics of S. Maria Maggiore," *Perennitas* (Festschrift Thomas Michels [Münster, 1963]), pp. 118ff., reprinted in Kantorowicz, *Selected Studies* (New York, 1965), pp. 25ff.

68. Grabar, *L'Empereur*, pp. 221ff. R. Krautheimer, "The Architecture of Sixtus III: A Fifth Century Renascence," *De Artibus Opuscula XL: Essays in Honor of Erwin Panofsky* (New York, 1961), pp. 291ff., especially p. 301f. Kantorowicz, "Puer Exoriens," p. 121f. U. Schubert, "Der politische Primatanspruch des Papstes dargestellt am Triumphbogen von Santa Maria Maggiore in Rom," *Kairos*, n.s. 13 (1971), pp. 594ff.

Fig. 22. Marriage of Moses. Rome, Santa Maria Maggiore. Mosaic

Fig. 23. Milan, Biblioteca Ambrosiana, cod. F. 205 P. Inf. (*Iliad*), fol. 39v

associations with the Roman past, but in this case primarily with the great epics. Scenes from the lives of Old Testament heroes are placed before the faithful in the guise of pages from a sumptuously illustrated manuscript of Homer or Vergil. The mosaicist makes a point of using settings, figure types, architectural motifs, and even frames that a contemporary beholder would associate with illustrations of the *Iliad* or *Aeneid*.[69]

No absolute line of demarcation can or need be drawn between scenes in the imperial and those in the epic mode. The same spirit informs the adoption of both. Thus, while some of the battle scenes in the Joshua sequence are composed in a manner comparable to the battle scenes in the Milan *Iliad* (cf. figs. 23 and 24),[70]

69. Cf. the literary efforts, undertaken as early as the fourth century, to recast books of the Old Testament in heroic meter (Socrates, Hist. eccl., 3, 16 [Migne, *P.G.*, 67, col. 417ff.]; Sozomenos, Church History, 5, 18 [ed. J. Bidez and G. C. Hansen, Die griechischen christlichen Schriftsteller 50, Berlin, 1960, p. 222]).

70. Karpp, *Mosaiken*, figs. 113, 153 (our fig. 24); cf., e.g., *Iliad*, pictures XXII, XXIX, XLII, XLIII (our fig. 23).

Fig. 24. Joshua Stays the Sun. Rome, Santa Maria Maggiore. Mosaic

the rendering of Joshua's defeat of the Amorite kings evidently was inspired by an imperial prototype such as the famous third-century sarcophagus in the Ludovisi Collection (cf. figs. 25 and 27).[71] Similarly, the arrangement of successive scenes of a narrative in two-register panels, a device for which again we found parallels in the Milan *Iliad* (fig. 21),[72] also has an interesting antecedent in the triumphal art of imperial Rome. On the Arch of Septimius Severus the sequences of scenes depicting—in the manner, and obviously in the tradition of the spiral bands of the Columns of Trajan and Marcus Aurelius—the emperor's military campaigns have been divided up so as to appear as superimposed strips in roughly square panels (fig. 26).[73] Thus the two-zone compositions at Santa Maria Maggiore, set like the reliefs on the Arch in a columnar framework,[74] may have evoked visual and mental associations with an imperial monument as well as with an illustrated epic.

How, then, are we to envisage the process whereby the mosaic cycle was created? It might still be argued that the bulk of the scenes were copied faithfully from an illuminated Bible and that for some of them models from other sources were substituted, mainly with a view to setting certain accents in relation to the topography of the building. But the dearth of close iconographic parallels in Old Testament illustrations even for those scenes at Santa Maria Maggiore that have the character of miniature paintings strongly argues against this. All indications are that the cycle as a whole was composed *ad hoc*; and that consequently the elements of miniature style are not in this case an automatic carry-over from book illumination.

The iconography of our mosaics was not, of course, created *ex nihilo*. General affinities with other Old Testament cycles do exist; and in at least one instance—the scene of the Stoning of Moses—a relationship to a lost Jewish prototype has been claimed.[75] But to account for such links it is sufficient to assume that the mosaics were designed under the direction of a knowledgeable adviser who drew up a list of subjects and prescribed the means of representation in general terms,

71. Karpp, *Mosaiken*, fig. 148. See Bianchi Bandinelli, *Hellenistic-Byzantine Miniatures*, p. 147f.; Kollwitz, "Josuazyklus," p. 107.

72. See note 56 above.

73. R. Brilliant, *The Arch of Septimius Severus in the Roman Forum*, Memoirs of the American Academy in Rome, vol. 29 (Rome, 1967), pls. 5f., 66ff., 76f., 86f. For the relationship of these reliefs to the spiral bands of the triumphal columns see pp. 219ff.; and R. Bianchi Bandinelli, *Rome: The Late Empire* (The Arts of Mankind, New York, 1971), pp. 66ff. Both Brilliant (p. 224) and Bianchi Bandinelli (p. 68) also make reference, à propos of the reliefs on the Arch, to the Old Testament mosaics at Santa Maria Maggiore.

74. For the original fifth-century setting of the mosaics, see Krautheimer, "The Architecture of Sixtus III," p. 291 and figs. 3, 4, 6.

75. Nordström, "Rabbinica" (see note 60 above), pp. 28ff.

perhaps only verbally or with the help of rough disposition sketches. Let it be recalled here that verbal instructions and cursory sketches were, in fact, the devices used to provide guidance in the execution of one of the picture cycles to which our mosaics are stylistically and chronologically close, namely, that of the Quedlinburg Itala.[76] In the realm of church decoration we even know of one instance in the fifth century where the painter is said to have done his work solely on the basis of verbal instructions.[77]

No doubt artists were able to implement such instructions, or flesh out sketches, with the help of an established and largely formulaic repertory of figures and scenery elements.[78] In the case of so big and important a project as the mosaic decoration of Santa Maria Maggiore, it is most likely that this was done "on paper" first. We may assume, in other words, that an *ad hoc* pictorial guide was prepared. But, granted that there was such a guide, and granted even that this guide was quite elaborate and thus prefigured many of those characteristic elements of the miniaturist's style that are so conspicuous in the mosaics, we still must conclude that these elements were not introduced mechanically but in full awareness of the monumental context for which the designs were destined and for which, it must be said, these miniature forms were not really suitable. As I have indicated, I would claim that these forms were brought to the fore deliberately and purposefully. The visual evocation of the epic mode was one of the means of stressing the ties of the Christian message with the Roman past.

Possibly the ideas in which these mosaics were rooted, the associations they were intended to evoke, soon ceased to be fully understood or appreciated. This

76. As Weitzmann has pointed out ("Book Illustration of the Fourth Century" [see note 58 above], p. 264), the miniaturist of the Quedlinburg leaves was not the first to represent subjects from the Books of Kings; witness the third-century frescoes of the Synagogue at Dura, which include scenes from these Books. Nevertheless, it must be assumed that the Quedlinburg miniatures were not copied from an earlier cycle but were composed afresh from stock elements, as Boeckler has shown (in Degering and Boeckler, *Italafragmente*, p. 153f.). The instructions to the painter written in the spaces reserved for the pictures and the use of generic descriptive terms in these instructions (e.g., "dux" for Abner) seem to me to prove this beyond any reasonable doubt. See also Boeckler's observation on Picture 3, where the miniaturist, by following the written instruction, has produced a representation somewhat at variance with the Bibilical text (ibid., p. 127). For the rough disposition sketches underlying some of the miniatures, see ibid. (pp. 72, 154 and pl. 8).

77. Gregory of Tours, History of the Franks, II, 17 (*Gregorii episcopi Turonensis Historiarum libri decem*, vol. 1, ed. R. Buchner, *Ausgewählte Quellen zur deutschen Geschichte des Mittelalters*, vol. 2 [Darmstadt, 1970], p. 98f.; cf. Davis-Weyer, *Early Medieval Art* [see note 26 above], p. 59).

78. For the use of conventional elements in narrative representations, see Boeckler in Degering and Boeckler, *Italafragmente*, pp. 150ff.; and Weitzmann, *Roll and Codex* (see note 39 above), pp. 154ff.

Fig. 25. Battle sarcophagus Ludovisi. Rome, Museo delle Terme

Fig. 26. Arch of Septimius Severus. Rome. Relief in northwest bay

Fig. 27. Defeat of the Amorites. Rome, Santa Maria Maggiore. Mosaic

may help to explain why these renderings of Old Testament subjects—to say nothing of the even more idiosyncratic presentation of New Testament subjects on the arch—not only have few tangible antecedents but also few tangible sequels.[79] When one thinks of the large number of works in a variety of media that to a greater or lesser extent are related, directly or indirectly, to another almost contemporary series of Old Testament scenes in Rome—the lost frescoes of the nave of San Paolo fuori le Mura—the contrast is striking. The San Paolo cycle clearly stood in the mainstream of Early Christian and medieval iconographic developments.[80] The mosaics of Santa Maria Maggiore—though equally accessible and likewise associated with one of the most venerable of Roman churches—were outside that mainstream from the start and remained so.

I shall venture a further observation. Not long ago there came to light another cycle of mosaics with Old Testament subjects that may be of much the same date as those of Santa Maria Maggiore. The cycle in question, which unfortunately is in very fragmentary condition, adorned the floor of a basilica uncovered in the 1950s at Mopsuestia in Cilicia.[81] It depicted in a single continuous band a series of scenes from the life of Samson accompanied by elaborate legends that paraphrased pertinent passages from the Septuagint version of the Book of Judges (figs. 28 and 30). I would suggest that in this case, too, there was an intention of evoking a visual association with an illuminated manuscript, though with a rotulus of the kind known to us through the Joshua Roll (fig. 29) rather than with a codex.[82] And here again there are indications that the bookish appearance of the decoration is not simply a result of mechanical copying from a manuscript source but was achieved by the designer of the mosaic independently and *ad hoc*.[83] Are such works perhaps symptomatic of a period in which proponents of pictorial imagery in religious buildings—still very much on the defensive—often

79. Cf. above, p. 128. A fragmentary scene on an ivory relief in Trier, plausibly attributed to the sixth century, has been related to the mosaic representing Abraham's encounter with Melchizedek and has been identified on the strength of this relationship; see *Frühchristliche Zeugnisse im Einzugsgebiet von Rhein und Mosel*, ed. T. K. Kempf and W. Reusch (Trier, 1965), p. 73f., no. 55 (with illustration and further references).

80. J. Garber, *Wirkungen der frühchristlichen Gemäldezyklen der alten Peters-und Paulsbasiliken in Rom* (Berlin and Vienna, 1918). O. Demus, *The Mosaics of Norman Sicily* (London, 1949), pp. 205f., 250ff. E. B. Garrison, *Studies in the History of Mediaeval Italian Painting*, vol. 4 (Florence, 1961), pp. 201ff.

81. L. Budde, *Antike Mosaiken in Kilikien*, vol 1 (Recklinghausen, 1969), pp. 67ff. and figs. 143–57; see also my review in *Art Bulletin* 55 (1973), pp. 140ff.

82. E. Kitzinger, "Observations on the Samson Floor at Mopsuestia," *Dumbarton Oaks Papers* 27 (1973), pp. 133ff.

83. Ibid., p. 143.

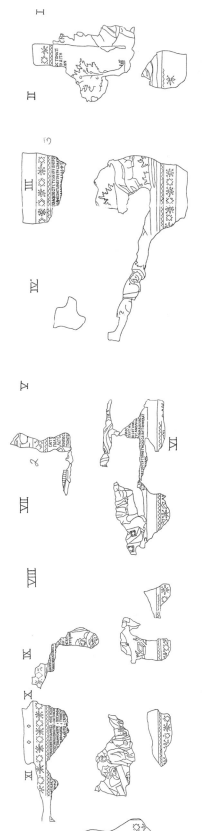

Fig. 28. Samson scenes. Misis (Mopsuestia), basilica. Floor mosaic (reconstruction by M. K. Donaldson)

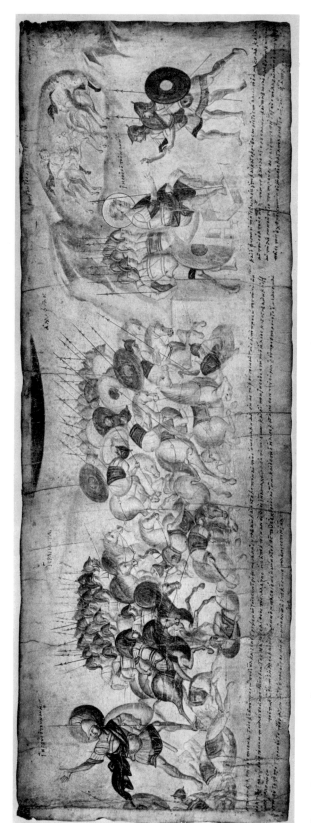

Fig. 29. Rome, Vatican Library, cod. Pal. gr. 431 (Joshua Rotulus), sheet XIII

Fig. 30. Samson scenes. Misis (Mopsuestia), basilica. Floor mosaic (detail)

cited the didactic value of such images and proclaimed them as equivalents of books, as γραφὴ σιωπῶσα, to quote Gregory of Nyssa?[84] The Mopsuestia Samson cycle, it is true, can hardly be called "silent." But an emphasis on the bookish character of representations in a Christian (or, in the case of Mopsuestia, possibly Jewish) house of worship could well be a sign of the times.

We have considered three different ways in which monumental paintings may be related to miniatures. One was the direct (or, probably more often, indirect) use of illustrations in library books as models; another, the use of miniature models

84. Migne, *P.G.*, 46, col. 757D. Cf. W. Elliger, *Die Stellung der alten Christen zu den Bildern in den ersten vier Jahrhunderten* (Leipzig, 1930), p. 65.

Fig. 31. Wall painting with simulated icons. Ohrid, Saint Sophia

especially prepared for the mosaicist or fresco painter and intended chiefly to provide him with iconographic guidance; finally we discussed instances of monumental decorations that have primarily a visual and formal relationship with book illuminations. Of these three categories, the second was probably the most common. Pictorial guides must have been in wide use among medieval muralists and must have been a normal link with the world of the illustrator. Examples of the first and the third categories, on the other hand, are relatively rare. That library books—and richly illustrated luxury volumes in particular—were not normally available to mural decorators is not surprising. As for the emphatically visual evocation of book art in mosaic or fresco, this may have been primarily a matter of special purposes and concerns and may have been confined to particular periods or circumstances. Certainly, in an overall view of Byzantine, or more generally medieval mural art, this element is not very conspicuous. It is probably true to say that when frescoes or mosaics belonging to the mature Middle Ages are visually evocative of another medium, that medium tends to be icon or panel painting (fig. 31) more often than book illumination.[85] But icons in turn—as Kurt Weitzmann has pointed out more than once—are intimately related to miniatures.[86] For a medieval beholder, mental associations with both media may well at times have merged.

85. See, for instance, the simulated portrait icons that form part of a number of medieval fresco decorations in the Balkans (fig. 31) and elsewhere (A. Grabar, *La peinture religieuse en Bulgarie* [Paris, 1928], pp. 64ff.). An example has recently come to light in Constantinople itself (C. L. Striker and Y. D. Kuban, "Work at Kalenderhane Camii in Istanbul: Second Preliminary Report," *Dumbarton Oaks Papers* 22 [1968], pp. 185ff., especially p. 190 and figs. 12–14). For mural ensembles of narrative scenes that in their compositional arrangement are reminiscent of icons, see Kitzinger, *Mosaics of Monreale*, figs. 44, 47, p. 102 n. 140; see also T. Velmans, "Les Fresques de Saint-Nicolas Orphanos à Salonique et les rapports entre la peinture d'icones et la decoration monumentale au XIVe siècle," *Cahiers Archéologiques* 16 (1966), pp. 145ff. Even a fresco decoration that seems to betray the hand of a miniaturist, as does that in the Saint Francis Chapel in the Kalenderhane Camii (Striker and Kuban, pp. 190ff. and figs. 19–29), may in fact be related to panel painting, as Professor Striker will demonstrate in his further publication on this important discovery.

86. K. Weitzmann, "Byzantine Miniature and Icon Painting in the Eleventh Century," *Proceedings of the XIIIth International Congress of Byzantine Studies, Oxford, 5–10 September, 1966* (London, 1967), pp. 207ff., especially pp. 213f., 217 (cf. idem, *Studies* [see note 58 above], pp. 271ff., especially pp. 282f., 293); idem, in *Icons from South Eastern Europe and Sinai* (London, 1968), p. XIII. Cf. the recent demonstration, on the basis of a contemporary source, that Pantoleon, the foremost of the eight illuminators of the Menologion of Basil II, was also highly regarded as a painter of icons (I. Ševčenko, "On Pantoleon the Painter," *Jahrbuch der Österreichischen Byzantinistik* 21 [1972], pp. 241ff.; Mango, *Art of the Byzantine Empire* [see note 34 above], p. 213f.).

Hugo Buchthal

Toward a History of
Palaeologan Illumination

A history of Palaeologan illumination has never been written, nor do I think that the time has come to make the attempt. What I propose to do here is to present rather tentatively some facts and ideas that may one day serve as stepping stones on the way to that task. Some may remain valid, others may well turn out to have been premature.[1]

There are several reasons for the neglect this subject has suffered until quite recently. In the fourteenth century, miniature painting generally no longer had the leading part it had held during the Middle Byzantine period; it had become a typical minor art following the lead of fresco and icon painting. It is only natural that it no longer attracted the most outstanding craftsmen, and that the variety of uses to which it was put were much more restricted than during the preceding centuries. In fact, the vast majority of Late Byzantine illuminated

1. This paper represents a first account of work carried out during my sabbatical year, 1971–72, with a generous grant from the John Simon Guggenheim Foundation, which allowed me to spend several months in Rome, to work in a number of other libraries in Western Europe, and, above all, to pay extended visits to Mount Sinai and Mount Athos.

I am grateful to the Chairman of the Department of Art and Archaeology of Princeton University, who asked me to contribute this lecture to the symposium held in April 1973, in honor of my friend Kurt Weitzmann. My debt to Kurt Weitzmann is self-evident; so is my profound obligation to Hans Belting, whose book, quoted in note 3, may be said to have started a new era in the study of Late Byzantine illumination, and who offered innumerable fruitful suggestions. As the lecture is here printed basically as it was delivered, the notes are restricted to essential bibliography and to references to miniatures that could not be reproduced in the present volume.

Fig. 1. Matthew. Mount Athos, Vatopedi,
cod. 938, fol. 18v

Fig. 2. Mark. Mount Athos, Vatopedi,
cod. 938, fol. 76v

manuscripts are just Gospel books with portraits of the four evangelists, and title
pieces at the beginning of the Gospel texts. Narrative scenes and cycles become the
exception rather than the rule. The surviving material is fairly abundant, but it
includes a considerable quantity of routine works of scant attraction and interest.
The vast majority is still unpublished, and the process of sifting has hardly begun.
Moreover, most of the material is not found in Western libraries but has remained
in the Greek East, especially in the various monasteries on Mount Athos. Professor
Weitzmann realized this many years ago and built up a unique collection of
photographs of Athos manuscripts, which he generously put at my disposal,
and which provided the starting point for my work in this field. From some points
of view this late material is easier to deal with than that from earlier centuries:
first, more manuscripts have been preserved than from earlier periods, and their
number is probably closer to that of the actual production; second, a fair number
of important manuscripts are securely dated. The obvious first task is to form small
groups of stylistically related miniatures, which can be assembled around one
or another of these dated manuscripts. It should not be expected that the result

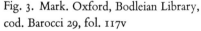

Fig. 3. Mark. Oxford, Bodleian Library,
cod. Barocci 29, fol. 117v

Fig. 4. John. Oxford, Bodleian Library,
cod. Barocci 29, fol. 276v

will amount to a continuous and consistent history of the illumination of the period. But it may serve as a nucleus and starting point for further research. What I shall do here is simply to present some of the more outstanding groups in loose association, and roughly in chronological order.

The distribution of illuminated manuscripts over the various scriptoria of Constantinople and some of the provincial cities and monasteries, on the other hand, presents a much more difficult problem than the mere establishment of a rough chronology. Thus, for instance, Thessaloniki, which always held a unique position in the Empire, must have played an important part in the book production of the period, just as it did in monumental painting. But this is one of the aspects of my subject with which I cannot deal here at all. I shall take it for granted that with very few exceptions the manuscripts discussed here were written and illuminated in Constantinople itself.

First, a few remarks on iconography are in order. We all know that the early Palaeologan period produced some extraordinarily faithful copies of Macedonian miniatures of the middle of the tenth century, not only in Psalter illustrations of the so-called aristocratic recension,[2] but also evangelist portraits.[3] However, one also finds new figural types that have no antecedents in earlier Byzantine art but that had been exceedingly popular in the Latin West all through the eleventh and twelfth centuries; there can be little doubt that they were borrowed from Western models. This is an interesting problem of wide implications, which I cannot discuss here in any detail; I hope to take it up again in a different context. I shall limit myself to illustrating one of these types, the evangelist, as a rule Matthew, who sharpens his pen (see fig. 1). The earliest surviving examples are securely dated in the years just before and after 1300.[4] Another new type that becomes common about this time, though it does not seem to depend on Western models, is the evangelist, usually Mark but sometimes also Luke, who holds an open book on his knees and with his left hand works on the book on the lectern with an eraser, as if he were left-handed (fig. 2). This type also appears about 1300,[5] is taken over into monumental painting,[6] and remains popular all through the fourteenth century.

The study of evangelist portraits of the Palaeologan period is in fact quite rewarding. There is, for instance, a standard set of four that recurs without the slightest change over a considerable period of time in over a dozen manuscripts that have otherwise nothing in common: not only the figural types, down to the smallest detail, but also the furniture (desks, tables) and architectural backgrounds remain identical throughout. The earliest dated instance occurs in a manuscript in Oxford[7] written by a known scribe who worked about 1300: Matthew sharpens his pen, Mark sits with his legs crossed and exhibits a scroll (fig. 3), Luke is shown writing—he is the only genuine Middle Byzantine type of the four—and John is

2. K. Weitzmann, "Eine Pariser-Psalter-Kopie des 13. Jahrhunderts auf dem Sinai," *Jahrbuch der Österreichischen Byzantinischen Gesellschaft* 6 (1957), pp. 125–43.

3. H. Belting, *Das illuminierte Buch in der spätbyzantinischen Gesellschaft*. Abhandlungen der Heidelberger Akademie der Wissenschaften, Philosophisch-historische Klasse, vol. 1 (Heidelberg, 1970), p. 9. H. Buchthal, "Notes on Some Early Palaeologan Miniatures," *Kunsthistorische Forschungen Otto Pächt zu seinem 70. Geburtstag* (Salzburg, 1972), pp. 36–43.

4. They are in: Oxford, Bodleian Library, Barocci 29, dated 1296–1318 (see *Greek Manuscripts in the Bodleian Library: An Exhibition held in Connection with the XIIIth International Congress of Byzantine Studies* [Oxford, 1966], no. 83), and Athos, Vatopedi 938, fol. 18v, dated 1304, reproduced in the present volume as fig. 1 (see also S. Eustratiades and Arcadios, *Catalogue of the Greek Manuscripts in the Library of the Monastery of Vatopedi on Mt. Athos* [Cambridge, Mass., 1924], p. 173).

5. The above-mentioned Gospel Vatopedi 938 is again one of the earliest instances. The miniature of Mark has been published in K. Weitzmann, *Studies in Classical and Byzantine Manuscript Illumination*, ed. H. L. Kessler (Chicago, 1971), fig. 320.

6. G. Millet, *Monuments de l'Athos* (Paris, 1927), pl. 36, 2.

7. Bodleian Library, Barocci 29 (see note 4 above). Belting, *Das illuminierte Buch*, p. 69.

seated before the cave of Patmos receiving the divine revelation (fig. 4). The iconographical tradition continues well into the fifteenth century; this may be demonstrated by two beautiful single leaves in the collection of Lord Clark of Saltwood.[8] Of the miniatures of this type that fall between these limits, some pose very intriguing problems. Thus, one set is found in a twelfth-century grand Lectionary of monumental proportions written for Constantinople, which has added Easter Tables dating from 1367, and this must also be the date when the four portraits were added on originally blank folios; evidently the Lectionary was then still in use, and was thought worthy to receive this elaborate figural decoration some two hundred years after it had been written.[9] Now there is in the same library—Lavra —a second set, on single leaves inserted one by one into an otherwise very ordinary fifteenth-century Gospel book written on paper.[10] The two sets are so close to each other from every point of view that they must belong to the same atelier tradition, and probably even to the same hand (cf. figs. 5 and 6): just compare the claw-like left hands in the miniatures of Matthew. The protraits of John, too, look almost like identical twins (figs. 7 and 8). I am not going to carry the comparison to greater detail now. Here is a problem one hardly ever encounters in Byzantine art of earlier periods; it is not easy, even with the originals in hand, to assign priority to one set or the other.

Next, let us examine an instance of the many new subjects taken from the liturgy: the Anapeson, the waking eye. Christ Emmanuel lies asleep in a paradisiacal landscape, a scene inspired by a passage in the 70th Psalm, read in the Easter Sunday service, and based on Jacob's Messianic prophecy in Genesis 49, which is interpreted according to the Physiologus: Christ, sleeping like a lion, with open eyes, may be asleep as a man but is awake as God. The presence of the Virgin underlines the significance of the image, which alludes to the work of Redemption made possible through Christ's Incarnation and Sacrifice. This is only one of the numerous subjects inspired by the liturgy that found their way into fourteenth-century church decoration; it occurs, among other places, in the frescoes of the Protaton,[11] of Lesnovo,[12] and of the Peribleptos of Mistra,[13] and belongs essentially to the realm of monumental art. Its presence in a Gospel manuscript of about 1300 in the Stauronikita monastery is, to the best of my knowledge, unique (fig. 9).[14]

8. *Masterpieces of Byzantine Art*, exhibition catalogue, Victoria and Albert Museum (London, 1958), nos. 213, 214; the miniature of Luke is reproduced in Alice Bank, "The Byzantine Exhibition," *Studio* 156 (1958), pp. 134–37, fig. 6.

9. Lavra A 113; see Spyridon and S. Eustratiades, *Catalogue of the Greek Manuscripts in the Library of the Lavra on Mt. Athos* (Cambridge, Mass., 1925), p. 12.

10. Lavra E 140; see ibid., p. 89 (no. 602).

11. Millet, *Monuments de l'Athos*, pl. 48, fig. 1.

12. G. Millet and T. Velmans, *La peinture du Moyen Age en Yougoslavie*, vol. 4 (Paris, 1969), fig. 41.

13. G. Millet, *Monuments byzantins de Mistra* (Paris, 1910), pl. 115, 1.

14. Stauronikita 45; cf. S. Lambros, *Catalogue of the Greek Manuscripts on Mount Athos*, vol. 1 (Cambridge, 1895), p. 77.

Fig. 5. Matthew. Mount Athos, Lavra, cod. A 113, fol. 48v

Fig. 6. Matthew. Mount Athos, Lavra, cod. E 140, fol. 13v

Fig. 7. John. Mount Athos, Lavra, cod. A 113, fol. 5v

Fig. 8. John. Mount Athos, Lavra, cod. E 140, fol. 235v

Fig. 9. The Anapeson. Mount Athos, Stauronikita, cod. 45,
fol. 12r

Another manuscript that I should like to single out for special attention is
the bilingual Greco-Latin Psalter in Berlin, in all probability a late-thirteenth-
century work with marginal illustrations by a Western hand copying those of a
Byzantine marginal Psalter, and with a French Calendar and Litany that seem
to have originated in Cyprus.[15] I include it here because it contains at the beginning
a separate quire with six full-page miniatures, which was not originally part of
the manuscript, and which in fact represents Constantinopolitan art at its best.
The cycle starts with the well-known miniature of a Byzantine aristocratic
family—unfortunately anonymous—venerating an icon of the Hodegetria,[16] and

15. Kupferstichkabinett 78 A 9; cf. P. Wescher, *Beschreibendes Verzeichnis der
Miniaturen-Handschriften und Einzelblätter des Kupferstichkabinetts der Staatlichen Museen
Berlin* (Leipzig, 1931), pp. 25–30; H. Böse, *Die lateinischen Handschriften der Sammlung
Hamilton zu Berlin* (Wiesbaden, 1966), pp. 66ff.

16. A. Grabar, *L'Iconoclasme byzantin* (Paris, 1957), fig. 1; Belting, *Illuminierte
Buch*, fig. 1.

Hugo Buchthal

Fig. 10. Scenes from the Life of David. Berlin, Staatliche Museen, Kupferstichkabinett, cod. 78 A 9, fol. 41v

ends with a portrait of David as King composing the Psalms. In between are four miniatures with scenes from David's life (see figs. 10 and 11). The beginning of the manuscript is the traditional place for such a cycle, as an extended frontispiece, in Psalters of the so-called aristocratic recension. In Psalters with marginal illustrations, on the other hand, as well as in a few manuscripts that occupy an intermediary position, such cycles are sometimes associated with the 151st Psalm, the last, supernumerary Psalm, in which David himself tells the story of his early life.[17] But these four leaves are the only instance known to me where the whole

17. S. Der Nersessian, *L'Illustration des psautiers grecs du Moyen Age, II: London Add. 19.352.* Bibliothèque des Cahiers Archéologiques, vol. 5 (Paris, 1970), pp. 99ff.

Fig. 11. Scenes from the Life of David. Berlin, Staatliche Museen,
Kupferstichkabinett, cod. 78 A 9, fol. 42r

cycle has been redesigned to form a literal illustration, verse by verse, of the 151st
Psalm, with the Greek and Latin texts added by later hands.[18] Unfortunately, we
do not know the original destination of these leaves, but it is perhaps significant
that in the fifteenth century the manuscript belonged to Carlotta, the last Lusignan
queen of Cyprus, who was a Palaeologina on her mother's side; the leaves may
have been a family heirloom. We may confidently ascribe them to one of the

18. Our figs. 10 and 11 reproduce fols. 41v and 42r; fols. 40 and 43 are reproduced
in Belting, *Illuminierte Buch*, figs. 2 and 3; the last miniature of the cycle, David Composing the Psalms, has come down to us in a very bad state of preservation.

leading ateliers in the capital in the late thirteenth century, perhaps even to the Hodegon monastery where the famous above-mentioned icon was kept.

The same Queen Carlotta owned two other manuscripts, which are now in the Vatican Library: the Gospel gr. 1158 and the *Praxapostolos* gr. 1208.[19] They are among the most accomplished masterpieces of Byzantine book production of any century; and they form the nucleus of a comprehensive and very homogeneous group of about fifteen manuscripts, including four that are written entirely in gold. All are certainly the products of the most resourceful and refined atelier in Constantinople about the year 1300, which was mainly patronized by an aristocratic clientele.[20] The Gospel in the Vatican has indeed Palaeologan monograms on two of its Canon Tables; and an almost identical Gospel manuscript, whose present whereabouts are unfortunately unknown, shows a similar, truly superior standard of script and ornament.[21] In the present context I want to show that the tradition established by this scriptorium can be traced well into the fourteenth century.[22] In some instances the connection is so close that one would like to assume direct copying. For example, the portrait of Matthew in yet another Vatican Gospel (fig. 12)[23]—a figural type not otherwise used for that evangelist— seems to be based directly on that of Luke, the author of Acts, in the *Praxapostolos* manuscript.[24] The two evangelists share not only the figural type and the very complicated system of folds, down to practically every single detail, but also some rather individual features: the inkpot is fastened to the evangelist's arm, and the scroll is, as it were, suspended in mid-air. But in the Gospel figure the development of style is carried further by several stages: the cascades of folds are at once simplified and hardened, and the loops of the mantle form an almost symmetrical pattern over the knees. While this manuscript, which should perhaps be dated in the 1320s, stands somewhat by itself, some others with portraits of seated evangelists form a more closely connected group. The first two we shall examine, Gospels in Lavra, cod. A 46, and Patmos, cod. 81, dated 1333 and 1335 respectively, were already recognized by Hans Belting as successors of the one with the Palaeo-

19. Belting, *Illuminierte Buch*, pp. 62–66, with earlier bibliography. Buchthal, "Notes" (see note 3 above), pp. 38ff.

20. The whole group of manuscripts will be the subject of a forthcoming monograph by Hans Belting and the author.

21. On the ornaments, see H. Buchthal, "Illuminations from an Early Palaeologan Scriptorium," *Jahrbuch der Österreichischen Byzantinistik* 21 (1972), Festschrift für Otto Demus zum 70. Geburtstag, pp. 47–56.

22. Belting, *Illuminierte Buch*, p. 67.

23. Vat. gr. 361; cf. *Il libro della Bibbia, Esposizione di manoscritti . . . Biblioteca Apostolica Vaticana* (Vatican City, 1972), no. 65.

24. For reproductions of the *Praxapostolos* miniature, see Belting, *Illuminierte Buch*, fig. 39; Buchthal, "Notes," fig. 6.

logan monograms and its relatives.[25] Mark in Patmos, a very individual creation,[26] presents a slight variation of the type found in the lost manuscript but he now holds a pen or an eraser in his left hand instead of only raising it to the lectern as in the model and in the tenth-century archetype, the codex Stauronikita 43[27]—an activity that I have mentioned before as a Palaeologan innovation. Moreover the evangelist is seated on the semicircular *thronos*, which in the earlier group is usually reserved for Luke or John. A comparison of the heads of the two figures of Mark[28] will best illustrate the revival of the atelier tradition after an interval of about thirty years.

The portrait of Matthew in the Patmos Gospels (fig. 13) invites almost equally close comparison with its counterpart in the lost manuscript (fig. 14). Here, however, it is not a matter of direct copying. The folds over the back and sleeve, as well as the type of the head, are indeed extremely similar. But when the miniature of the same evangelist in the just-mentioned sister manuscript in Lavra is introduced into the discussion (fig. 15), it will be seen that the Patmos and Lavra portraits share a number of features that cannot be traced back to the lost manuscript. In both later works the book is held more closely to the body, so that the left knee becomes visible; the left foot, on the other hand, is now almost hidden by the drapery, and there is a lectern, which is missing in the archetype. Another common feature is the modeling of the folds of the drapery on the right thigh in a series of vertical lines. The inevitable conclusion is that both miniatures depend directly on a lost model which already contained all the characteristics that they share. This model can have preceded them by only a few years: Hans Belting has shown that the architectural framework in the Lavra miniature, which recurs identically in the portrait of Mark in Patmos, is copied directly from a Kariye Djami mosaic.[29] Thus the two manuscripts in Lavra and Patmos dated 1333 and 1335 emerge from their isolation: they were preceded, if only by a few years, by other, equally important work. That work was based on models that were about one generation older, of the kind of the lost and the Vatican Gospels, cod. gr. 1158. The soft-spoken Hellenism of the archetype has given way to an almost metallic glitter, the naturally bulging drapery is transformed into hard segmentation, and the easily inclined attitude of the writing author is replaced by unbending stiffness. The manuscripts in Lavra and Patmos are almost twins, of practically the same size, sharing practically all codicological characteristics, and with similar scripts and headpieces. But it is also clear that the Patmos copy is the more ambitious of the two. It is indeed the result of a very special effort. Witness the setting, the grandiose architectural background, and the elaborate frame, absent from all

25. Belting, *Illuminierte Buch*, p. 67.
26. Ibid., fig. 42, n. 233.
27. For the archetype, see Buchthal, "Notes," p. 36 and fig. 4.
28. Belting, *Illuminierte Buch*, figs. 37 and 42.
29. Ibid., p. 67.

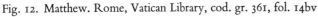

Fig. 12. Matthew. Rome, Vatican Library, cod. gr. 361, fol. 14bv

Fig. 13. Matthew. Patmos, Monastery of Saint John, cod. 81, fol. 16v

late-thirteenth-century models but prominently present in the tenth-century archetypes of the kind of the Stauronikita Gospels cod. 43. In this we may recognize a last hesitant attempt to revive the magnificence and the deluxe character of Macedonian illumination. The Lavra miniature is not of quite the same high quality, the execution is cruder, the chrysography on the table is somewhat coarse, and the columns that ought to support the framing pediment—and do support it in the Patmos miniature of Mark[30]—have been omitted. Considering that the Patmos evangelist is actually the younger of the two by two years, there can be no question of direct dependence. Moreover, in the Patmos manuscript the first page of each Gospel is written in gold, and the headpieces at the beginning of the single Gospels are much more elaborate (see fig. 16). The title headings in the Lavra codex seem to be the work of the illuminator, not that of an experienced scribe (see fig. 17). Those in Patmos are not only much more elegantly written,

30. Ibid., fig. 42.

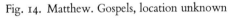

Fig. 14. Matthew. Gospels, location unknown   Fig. 15. Matthew. Mount Athos, Lavra, cod. A 46, fol. 16v

but also refer in some cases not to the Gospels themselves, but to the Sunday readings for which the first chapters of the relevant Gospels served. This one would not normally find in a complete Gospel book, but only in a Lectionary. The usual procedure, which was also followed in the Lavra Gospels, was to add these liturgical indications, if they were required at all, on the top of the page. Obviously the Patmos manuscript was, from the beginning, intended for liturgical use, perhaps by an eminent prelate. It is one of the finest of all surviving fourteenth-century manuscripts; we are indeed fortunate that it is precisely dated, and that we can assign it its exact place in the Palaeologan development.

The story can be carried still further. Luke in the Patmos Gospel (fig. 18) has the plain wooden seat and cross-footed lectern of Mark in the lost manuscript,[31] the same manuscript that also contained the archetypes of the Patmos portraits of Matthew and Mark. The architectural setting here consists of an architrave supported by a colonnade, and a two-storied building with sloping roofs and twin

31. Ibid., fig. 37.

Fig. 16. Beginning of Gospel of Saint Mark.
Patmos, Monastery of Saint John, cod. 81, fol. 99r

Fig. 17. Beginning of Gospel of Saint Luke.
Mount Athos, Lavra, cod. A 46, fol. 175r

windows. The same very specific background recurs in a number of other manuscripts: first, Matthew in a Gospel in Grottaferrata (fig. 19),[32] who does not write
but exhibits a billowing scroll. The table and the lectern with its cruciform
stand also recur. The mottled columns are shorter and thicker, and the coffered
ceiling of the colonnade is more clearly visible. The two figures themselves do
not show any specific similarities; the miniatures may not even be the work
of the same atelier. Still, they are close enough to be attributed to roughly the
same period.

The Grottaferrata evangelists are, in turn, related to the portraits in a Gospel
in the Byzantine Museum in Athens,[33] which are unfortunately badly preserved.

32. A. Rocchi, *Codices cryptenses* (Tuscolo, 1883), pp. 2–4. A. Muñoz, *L'Art
byzantin à l'exposition de Grottaferrata* (Rome, 1906), fig. 49. M. Bonicatti, "Miniatura
bizantina ed italogreca in alcuni codici della Badia di Grottaferrata," *Accademie e biblio-
teche d'Italia* 25 (1957), pp. 107–22, especially p. 114, figs. 5, 6.
33. Δημητρίου Πάλλα κατάλογος χειρογράφων τοῦ Βυζαντινοῦ Μουσείου
Ἀθηνῶν, μέρος τρίτον (Athens, 1955), pp. 37ff.

A comparison of the seats, the tables, the lectern, and the ornaments on the architraves of the buildings in the two miniatures of Matthew (figs. 19 and 20) will illustrate the connection; and the two heads are so similar that one is tempted to attribute them to the same master. A juxtaposition of the pictures of Mark in the two manuscripts will lead to the same conclusion.[34] But more important is the fact that the characteristic background of Luke in Patmos and Matthew in Grottaferrata recurs in the author portrait of a Climacus manuscript in the Athos monastery of Stauronikita, cod. 50[35]—one of the very few fourteenth-century manuscripts with a cycle of text illustrations. The cycle as a whole is based directly on that of a late-eleventh-century Climacus manuscript in the Vatican;[36] but this does not apply to the author portrait, which is, as it were, brought up to date, and repeats many features of the Grottaferrata evangelist, including the billowing scroll and the coffered ceiling. On this evidence, the portrait, and the whole narrative cycle, which is by the same hand, may be dated into the second quarter of the century, and probably even more precisely in the 1330s, just as the Gospels in Lavra and Patmos. It is moreover interesting to observe that some features of this group of manuscripts, specifically the architectural backgrounds, the colonnade, and also the pediment inspired by the Kariye Djami mosaic, recur in a manuscript that belongs to the second half, probably even to the end of the century.[37] It would appear that the second quarter of the century set a standard that remained valid for many decades.

The comparatively close connection that exists between the miniatures of all these manuscripts—the Gospel books in Patmos and Lavra, Grottaferrata and Athens, and the Climacus in Stauronikita—contrasts forcefully with the difference one finds in a roughly contemporary group of manuscripts that were all written by a certain Chariton, who was a monk in the monastery τῶν Ὁδηγῶν, and who signed eleven codices with the same elaborate formula: Θεοῦ τὸ δῶρον καὶ Χαρίτονος

---

34. The Athens miniature of Mark is unfortunately too badly preserved to be reproduced. For the Grottaferrata miniature, see Muñoz, *L'Art byzantin*, fig. 50.

35. J. R. Martin, *The Illustration of the Heavenly Ladder of John Climacus* (Princeton, 1954), fig. 135. The similarities of the Patmos and Climacus miniatures have already been noticed by Bonicatti, "Aspetti dell'industria libraria mediobizantina negli scriptoria italogreci e considerazioni su alcuni manoscritti criptensi miniati," *Atti del 3 Congresso internazionale di Studi sull'alto Medio Evo* (Spoleto, 1959), p. 353.

36. Martin, op. cit., p. 164.

37. Formerly in the Dyson Perrins Collection; see Sir George Warner, *Descriptive Catalogue of Illuminated Manuscripts in the Library of C. W. Dyson Perrins* (Oxford, 1920), no. 130; Sotheby catalogue, *The Dyson Perrins Collection*, part 3, 29 November 1960, lot 113.

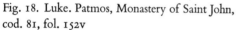

Fig. 18. Luke. Patmos, Monastery of Saint John,
cod. 81, fol. 152v

Fig. 19. Matthew. Grottaferrata, Badia,
cod. A α II, fol. 15v

πόνος; in most instances he also gave the date of their completion.[38] Unfortunately only one of them, which has not yet been photographed and which I have not been able to see,[39] has figural miniatures; and only five others have illuminated ornaments. I shall illustrate three of them: the first is a page from a Lectionary in Paris dated 1336 (fig. 21);[40] the second is from a Gospel book in Lavra dated 1342 (fig. 22)[41]—this page is beautifully finished in two colors only, blue and gold, and in this respect is a successor of the headpieces in the Vatican

38. L. Politis, "Eine Schreiberschule im Kloster τῶν Ὁδηγῶν, part 2, *Byzantinische Zeitschrift* 51 (1958), pp. 261–87.

39. Ibid., p. 262, no. 2. The manuscript that Politis lists as Iviron 505 is not included in Lambros's catalogue (see note 14 above).

40. Ibid., p. 263, no. 7. Ebersolt, *La Miniature byzantine* (Paris, 1926), pl. 67, fig. 1.

41. Politis, "Schreiberschule," no. 8. Spyridon and Eustratiades, *Catalogue* (see note 9 above), p. 8 (A 67).

Fig. 20. Matthew. Athens, Byzantine Museum, cod. 157, fol. 30r

Gospels cod. gr. 1158 with the Palaeologan monograms;[42] the third, the most outstanding manuscript of the group, is a Psalter written in 1346 for the Empress Anna, the widow of Andronicus III, with a magnificent title ornament again executed in blue and gold (fig. 23).[43] The art historian has reluctantly to admit he would never have guessed that these three manuscripts were illuminated in the same scriptorium and within a few years of each other. They are all of absolutely stunning quality, to which our black-and-white reproductions can hardly

42. Buchthal, "Illuminations" (see note 21 above), fig. 6.
43. Iviron 1384; cf. Lambros, *Catalogue*, vol. 2 (1900), p. 279.

Fig. 21. Beginning of Lectionary. Paris, Bibliothèque Nationale, cod. gr. 311, fol. 1r

Fig. 22. Beginning of Gospel of Saint John. Mount Athos, Lavra, cod. A 67, fol. 267r

Fig. 23. Beginning of Psalter. Mount Athos, Iviron, cod. 1384, fol. 1r

Fig. 24. Beginning of fourteenth homily. Paris, Bibliothèque Nationale, cod. gr. 543, fol. 289r

do justice. But they are obviously not connected by any easily recognizable atelier tradition. It is even more disconcerting to find that the ornamental headpieces in the Paris Lectionary of 1336 (fig. 21) are extraordinarily similar in style to those of the Paris manuscript of Gregory Nazianzenus, gr. 543 (fig. 24),[44] which was most certainly written by a different scribe, and probably in a different scriptorium. But the comparison, whatever it may be worth, encourages me to attribute the Gregory manuscript to the 1330s. That date may moreover be confirmed through the comparison of another headpiece in the Gregory manuscript (fig. 25) with a charming miniature in a Gospel in Pistoia, dated 1330 (fig. 26),[45] in which there is a very similar feeling for the measured pace and the ornamental effect of the rinceaux. The influence of Islamic ornament that gives most of these headpieces their particular identity has never received the attention it deserves; it is strikingly confirmed when one turns to two other miniatures in the Pistoia manuscript in which the evangelists are completely surrounded by luxurious thickets of floral patterns (figs. 27 and 28).

Along with the Stauronikita Climacus, the Gregory is one of the very few fourteenth-century manuscripts with a cycle of narrative miniatures: there is, or was, one at the beginning of each sermon. They are all full page and thus physically independent of the text.[46] But most of them are in the middle of their respective gatherings on verso folios that have the end of the text of the preceding homily on the recto; in other words, they were executed in the scriptorium, and together with text and ornament. These miniatures again represent a very special effort, and to the superficial observer they look splendid enough.[47] They certainly show a high degree of technical perfection. But this will not deceive us about the somewhat pedestrian compositions, the dry execution, the lack of vitality, the absence of creative power; the excellence of their workmanship only serves to underline their poverty of grace and emotional appeal. It is true that a few miniatures are less drab and more distinguished than the others. But generally speaking, the manuscript demonstrates quite clearly the superiority of ornament over figural miniatures; the regeneration that the illuminations owe to the influence of Islamic ornament has no parallel in the figural work, most of which simply represents an impoverished version of century-old formulas.[48]

44. Ebersolt, *Miniature*, pls. 66, 70.

45. *Mostra storica nazionale della miniatura, Roma*, exhibition catalogue (Florence, 1953), no. 24. A. Turyn, *Dated Greek Manuscripts of the Thirteenth and Fourteenth Centuries in the Libraries of Italy* (Urbana-Chicago-London, 1972), pp. 176ff., with bibliography.

46. Belting, *Illuminierte Buch*, p. 10.

47. H. Omont, *Miniatures des plus anciens manuscrits grecs de la Bibliothèque Nationale* (Paris, 1929), pls. 119–25. G. Galavaris, *The Illustrations of the Liturgical Homilies of Gregory Nazianzenus* (Princeton, 1969), pls. 103–10.

48. According to the *stemma* in Galavaris, op. cit., p. 193 this manuscript should be traced back directly to the archetype of the liturgical recension.

Fig. 25. Beginning of thirteenth homily. Paris, Bibliothèque Nationale, cod. gr. 543, fol. 261r

The principal dated manuscript from the following decade—the forties—is a Gospel of 1346 in the monastery of Saint Catherine on Mount Sinai, which mentions as donor Isaac Asen, a grandson of Michael VIII.[49] Again, the very pretentious display of the evangelist portraits (fig. 29) and the virtuosity of their execution are in strange contrast to the monotony of the compositional scheme,

49. Sinai 152; see Belting, *Illuminierte Buch*, p. 58, with bibliography; K. Weitzmann, *Illustrated Manuscripts at St. Catherine's Monastery on Mt. Sinai*, Medieval and Renaissance Studies, The Monastic Microfilm Library, St. John's University (Collegeville, Minn., 1973), p. 29, fig. 4.

Fig. 26. Mark. Pistoia, Biblioteca Fabroniana, cod. 307, fol. 101r

which is repeated almost identically in all four miniatures with a lack of subtlety and with an insensitive accumulation of heterogeneous drapery motifs. Their most redeeming feature is the unusual color scheme. This style is actually a desiccated version of that of the 1320s. The master must have been thoroughly familiar with the Kariye Djami frescoes, but shows little understanding of their human message (fig. 30).[50] It is a sad reflection, and, as I believe, characteristic of

50. P. A. Underwood, *The Kariye Djami*, vol. 3 (New York, 1966), pl. 364.

Fig. 27. Luke. Pistoia, Biblioteca Fabroniana, cod. 307, fol. 157r

Fig. 28. John. Pistoia, Biblioteca Fabroniana, cod. 307, fol. 247r

that particular decade, that one of the leading political figures of the period[51] should not have been able to command the services of a more versatile artist.

During the second half of the century the Hodegon monastery comes again into prominence, through the works of a monk by the name of Joasaph,[52] whose activities as a scribe can be traced in thirty signed and dated manuscripts ranging in date from 1360 to 1405, all of them scriptural texts and theological and liturgical works. During the later part of his life he was Higoumenos of his monastery, and the known date of his death, November 1406,[53] fits in well with the evidence afforded by the dated manuscripts. The subscriptions all have the same formula as those in the Chariton manuscripts: Θεοῦ τὸ δῶρον καὶ ᾿Ιωᾶσαφ πόνος. But few have illuminated ornaments, and only one has figural miniatures: the well-known Kantakouzenos manuscript in Paris, dated 1371–75.[54] And once again, just as in the case of the Chariton manuscripts, a survey of the illuminations will not indicate a common workshop tradition. As proof of this, the headpieces on the first pages of a Gospel in the British Museum dated 1366 (see fig. 31)[55] may be compared with one in a *Praxapostolos* in the Vatican dated 1394 (fig. 32),[56] a particularly beautiful specimen written and illuminated with special care, and on parchment of the finest quality. While Joasaph's script remains practically unchanged over the years, the ornaments alone would not justify the attribution of the manuscripts to the same scriptorium.

Three full-page miniatures in the Kantakouzenos manuscript represent the Council of 1351, the double portrait of the author as emperor and monk,[57] and the Transfiguration, the focal image of the Hesychast doctrine (fig. 33).[58] All three are painted on ruled pages in the middle of their respective gatherings; they must have been produced in the monastery itself and in close collaboration with the scribe. They should be studied together with the illustrations of two other

51. On Isaac Asen, see D. Nicol, *The Byzantine Family of Kantakouzenos*, Dumbarton Oaks Studies, vol. 11 (Washington, D.C., 1968), pp. 47ff.

52. Politis, "Schreiberschule," part 1, pp. 19ff.

53. H. Hunger, "Johannes Chortasmenos, ein Byzantinischer Intellektueller der Paläologenzeit," *Wiener Studien* 70 (1957), Festschrift K. Mras, pp. 153–63.

54. Bib. Nat. cod. gr. 1242; bibliography in Belting, *Illuminierte Buch*, p. 52, n. 169.

55. Burney 18; see Politis, "Schreiberschule," part 1, p. 27, no. 2.

56. Chigi R. V. 29; ibid., p. 31, no. 25. Bibliography in P. Canart and V. Peri, *Sussidi bibliografici per i manoscritti greci della Biblioteca Vaticana*, Studi e Testi 261 (Vatican City, 1970), p. 175.

57. See Belting, *Illuminierte Buch*, fig. 51, pp. 84ff., on the theological significance of the double portrait.

58. Ibid., fig. 11, pp. 15ff.

Fig. 29. Matthew. Mount Sinai, cod. gr. 152, fol. 16v

manuscripts, a Lectionary in Koutloumousi on Mount Athos[59] with only one miniature—of Saint John (fig. 34)—and several illuminated headpieces (see fig. 35), and a Gospel in the Vatican with portraits of all four evangelists (figs. 36–39) but no ornaments. These two codices have no signatures, but they are clearly written by one scribe, and in a hand very similar to that in the Kantakouzenos manu-

59. Koutloumousi 62; see Lambros, *Catalogue*, vol 1, p. 280; P. Huber, *Athos. Leben, Glaube, Kunst* (Zürich and Freiburg, 1969), fig. 130. S. M. Pelekanidis et al., *The Treasures of Mount Athos, Illuminated Manuscripts*, I (Athens, 1974), p. 453, figs. 306–10.

Fig. 30. Raising of the Daughter of Jairus. Istanbul, Kariye Djami. Fresco

script[60] and its relatives; whether or not by Joasaph himself, the script is certainly enough alike to attribute both of them to the Hodegon monastery. In any case, it appears that Joasaph did not sign every manuscript he wrote; recently the unsigned and undated Moscow copy of the *Akathistos* Hymn has been attributed to his pen.[61] It is true that the headpieces in the Koutloumousi Lectionary again

60. For a specimen of the text of Paris gr. 1242, see H. Omont, *Fac-similés des manuscrits grecs datés de la Bibliothèque Nationale* (Paris, 1891), pl. 95.

61. G. M. Proxorov, "A Codicological Analysis of the Illuminated *Akathistos* to the Virgin," *Dumbarton Oaks Papers* 26 (1972), p. 242.

Fig. 31. Beginning of Gospel of Saint Matthew. London, British Museum, cod. Burney 18, fol. 3r

Fig. 32. Beginning of *Praxapostolos*. Rome, Vatican Library, cod. Chigi R. V. 29, fol. 1r

have no specific similarities with those in other manuscripts from the scriptorium. But I think no detailed analysis is necessary to make the point that the two portraits of Saint John (figs. 34 and 39) are the work of one and the same master. The placidity and flabbiness of the figures, the loose-hanging draperies with their fishbone-pattern folds, the sling over the right arm, the distribution of the highlights, the exaggerated roundness near the thighs, the white lines following the contours of the back and ending in right angles may be mentioned, as well as the formation of head, hair and beard, the carvings and parallel shadings of furniture and footstool, the identical writing utensils on the table. The near-identity of the captions in the two miniatures also deserves attention, the letters as well as the flourishes. To a lesser degree, the Lectionary miniature may also be compared with the other portraits in the Gospels; thus, the strange elliptical outline of the back of the figure of Matthew (fig. 36), and the very close similarity of the lower part of the figure, with the same complicated system of folds, in the miniature of Luke (fig. 38). Moreover, the color scheme in all these miniatures is identical.[62]

My main point, however, is that not only the evangelist portraits in these two unsigned and undated manuscripts are by the same hand. I think that the miniatures in the Kantakouzenos manuscript, as well, should be attributed to the same master. It is, of course, only the Biblical scenes that lend themselves to a detailed comparison. But their style may be described in exactly the same terms that applied to the evangelist portraits: the flabbiness and wavy outlines of the figures, the ample drapery, the folds and highlights; the neckline of Moses (fig. 33, top right) and Luke (fig. 38); the heads of Mark (fig. 37) and James (fig. 33, bottom right); the formation of the hands; the eyes; and finally, the color scheme, including the turquoise color of the ground in the evangelist portraits, which recurs in the Trinity scene of the Kantakouzenos manuscript.[63] We may assume that not only were all three manuscripts written in the same Constantinopolitan monastery, that of the Hodegon, but also that their miniatures are the work of one illuminator. This master, who received official commissions and who worked in one of the leading scriptoria of the capital, must have been one of the most renowned of his time; and it is his style that reappears some years later in a slightly more developed form in the manuscripts illuminated by Theophanes the Greek and his followers in Russia (fig. 40).[64]

The dating of the Gospel and Lectionary miniatures in the third quarter of

62. Color reproductions of the double portrait in Paris gr. 1242 in A. Grabar, *Byzantine Painting* (Geneva, 1953), p. 184; of the Transfiguration miniature in I. Hutter, *Early Christian and Byzantine Art* (New York, 1971), pl. 181; of the Koutloumousi portrait in Pelekanidis et al., *Treasures of Mount Athos*, fig. 306.

63. See the color reproduction in Grabar, *Byzantine Painting*, p. 184.

64. V. Lazarev, *Theophanes der Grieche und seine Schule* (Vienna and Munich, 1968), fig. 109.

Fig. 33. Transfiguration. Paris, Bibliothèque Nationale, cod. gr. 1242, fol. 92v

Fig. 34. John. Mount Athos, Koutloumousi, cod. 62, fol. 3v

Fig. 35. Beginning of Lectionary. Mount Athos,
Koutloumousi, cod. 62, fol. 4r

the century (when the Kantakouzenos manuscript was completed) is moreover
confirmed by the fact that they represent the same stage of development of Palaeologan style as the frescoes of the Church of the Peribleptos in Mistra. No detailed
demonstration is possible here; only a few examples can be mentioned. The
Prophets of the cupola[65] have the same proportions, the same flabbiness, the same
bizarre rounded contours, the thickening toward the waist, the same treatment of
loose-hanging draperies, the same dented facial outlines (figs. 41 and 42). A head
from the Passion scenes in Mistra[66] may be compared with that of an evangelist
from the Vatican Gospel (fig. 36). Finally, the two figures of Christ of the Transfiguration in Mistra[67] and in the Kantakouzenos manuscript[68] are so close that

65. Ντ. Μουρίκη, ''Αἱ βιβλικαὶ προεικονίσεις τῆς Παναγίας εἰς τὸν τροῦλλον τῆς
Περιβλέπτου τοῦ Μυστρᾶ,'' Ἀρχαιολογικὸν Δελτίον 25 (1970), pp. 217–51, pls. 71–93.

66. D. Talbot Rice, *Byzantine Painting: The Last Phase* (London, 1968), fig. 150.

67. Ibid., fig. 144.

68. Cf. the enlarged photo in A. Grabar, *Miniatures byzantines de la Bibliothèque
Nationale* (Paris, 1939), fig. 60.

Fig. 36. Matthew. Rome, Vatican Library,
cod. gr. 1160, fol. 24v

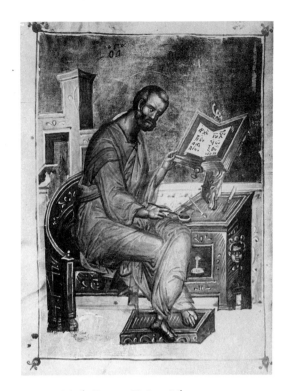

Fig. 37. Mark. Rome, Vatican Library,
cod. gr. 1160, fol. 67v

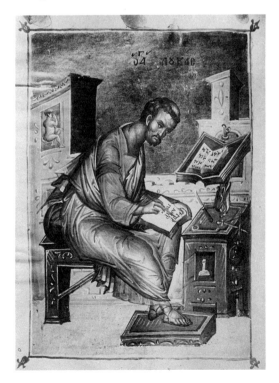

Fig. 38. Luke. Rome, Vatican Library,
cod. gr. 1160, fol. 100v

Fig. 39. John. Rome, Vatican Library,
cod. gr. 1160, fol. 154v

Fig. 40. John and Prochoros. Moscow, Lenin Library, cod. 8657, fol. 2v

Fig. 41. Prophet Nahum. Mistra, Peribleptos.
Cupola fresco

Fig. 42. Prophet Zechariah. Mistra,
Peribleptos. Cupola fresco

they are almost interchangeable. It is well to remember in this connection that the Peribleptos frescoes are usually attributed to a metropolitan, Constantinopolitan school;[69] and also that precisely during this period Manuel Kantakouzenos, the second son of the deposed emperor, resided in Mistra as despot of the Morea (1349–80).[70]

It may appear presumptuous to draw far-reaching conclusions from these examples, which were chosen partly because they represent the aristocratic tradition of

69. C. Delvoye, "Mistra," *Corsi di cultura sull'arte ravennate e bizantina* (1964), p. 129.

70. Nicol, *Kantakouzenos* (see note 51 above), p. 123.

Constantinople, but partly as well because good photographs are available. Still, I think they may be fairly representative of the main lines of development. Like the artists in the period immediately after Iconoclasm, illuminators after 1261 turned first of all to models of an earlier age, from the period before the catastrophe. There certainly was some continuity through the period of the Latin occupation,[71] but it was necessarily restricted. One of its results was the introduction of some Latin iconographical types, an aspect on which further research is needed. But the grand aristocratic tradition reverted first and foremost to models dating from the middle of the tenth century, the period of the Macedonian Renaissance. In comparison to earlier centuries there is a severe reduction in range of subject matter, but no lack of originality. Inevitably there is a great deal of repetition of conventional formulas. But in the best work of the period the traditional material has acquired new life and vigor, and original and sometimes even daring solutions are explored. Some of the evangelist portraits and illuminated headpieces may be counted among the finest products of Constantinopolitan art. Moreover, just as in the eleventh century, new subjects and whole new cycles, which owe their inspiration to the liturgy, appear.[72] The tradition established at the turn of the thirteenth to the fourteenth century is taken up again a generation later, gradually turning from an imitation of Hellenistic to a more hieratic style, probably under the influence of icon painting. It appears that this decade—the 1330s—represents the highlight of the entire development: this must have been a period of renewed creative activity in Constantinople. It is also to that decade that the two best-known manuscripts of the century with cycles of narrative miniatures seem to belong: the Gregory in Paris and the Climacus in Stauronikita. But as a rule complex compositional schemes are eschewed; and in those rare instances where they are attempted they display a certain poverty of ideas and lack of vitality and tension, in strange contrast to the pretentious layout and the high standard of craftsmanship. The gradual decline of what was once a great art becomes painfully evident. It is mainly the illuminated ornament that stands out in these manuscripts, drawing on Islamic models for new strength and for a wealth of new ideas. Here is a fruitful subject for further investigation.

The decisive break occurs in the 1340s, the decade of the civil war, the most savage and destructive of its kind in the long history of Byzantium; and it appears that in a sense book illumination never completely recovered. There is a drop not

71. K. Weitzmann, "Constantinopolitan Book Illumination in the Period of the Latin Conquest," *Gazette des Beaux-Arts* 86 (1944), pp. 193–214; reprinted in *Studies* (see note 5 above), pp. 314–34.

72. The best-known instance is the illustration of the Akathistos Hymn; see T. Velmans, "Une Illustration inédite de l'Acathiste et l'iconographie des hymnes liturgiques à Byzance," *Cahiers Archéologiques* 22 (1972), pp. 131–65; V. D. Lixačeva, "The Illumination of the Greek Manuscript of the *Akathistos* Hymn," *Dumbarton Oaks Papers* 26 (1972), pp. 255–62.

only in the number of manuscripts singled out for illustration, but especially in their quality. It is significant that most of the manuscripts from the third quarter of the century that any impartial observer would pick out as the finest and most accomplished books of their kind have turned out to come from the same scriptorium, that of the Hodegon monastery, and that at least three of them are the work of one and the same master.

Still, the role of the Hodegon monastery is far from clear. It is true that its activities can be traced practically without interruption through three quarters of a century. It accepted imperial commissions from a Palaeologan dowager empress and, a quarter of a century later, from her deadly antagonist and rival, the already deposed emperor John VI. There can be no doubt about its leading part in the history of fourteenth-century book production. But very few of the preserved manuscripts are illuminated. Most of the ornamental work is on a very high level, but it does not bear out the existence of an atelier tradition. It appears that illuminators were brought in from outside whenever their services were required. Here, too, further research is needed.

Finally, the connections between illumination and fresco and icon painting deserve more attention. I have mentioned one or two instances, but of course there are others. And as so many manuscripts are securely dated, these connections may one day help us to assign more precise dates to some outstanding fourteenth-century icons.

Note: Figs. 2, 5, 6, 7, 8, 9, 15, 17, 22, and 23 are reproduced by special permission of the Patriarchal Institute for Patristic Studies, Thessaloniki.

Index